English 7 – 14
Every Child's Entitlement

English 7-14

Every Child's Entitlement

edited by

Viv Edwards
Jagiro Goodwin
Angela Wellings

David Fulton Publishers

London

David Fulton Publishers Ltd
2 Barbon Close, London WC 1N 3JX

First published in Great Britain by
David Fulton Publishers 1991

Note: The right of the contributors to be identified as the authors of their work has been asserted by them in accordance with the Copyright, Designs and Patents Act 1988.

British Library Cataloguing in Publication Data
English 7 – 14 every child's entitlement.
1. Primary Schools. Curriculum: English language 2.
Great Britain
I Edwards, Viv II Goodwin, Jagiro III Wellings, Angela
372. 60440941

ISBN 1–85346–157–1

Designed by Almac Ltd, London
Typeset by Page One Communications, Reading
Printed in Great Britain by Bell and Bain Ltd, Glasgow

Contents

Acknowledgements

We would like to thank the staff and pupils of Arbour Vale School, Katesgrove Primary School, Redlands Primary School, Wilson Road Primary School and Prospect School for the various examples of work and the quotations used throughout this book. Thanks also to Audrey Gregory for permission to reproduce the example of children's writing on p51, to Shelagh Hubbard for the example on p.53, to Robin Richardson for the example on page 54, to Saroj Mistry for the flow chart on page 81 and to Roy Yates for 'Spot Starts School Today!' on page 30. We would like to acknowledge Janet Page's helpful comments on the specific needs of isolated bilingual children in outlying schools and Lib Taylor for her advice on drama. Finally, thanks to Berkshire Education Multicultural Services Resource Unit for the photographs on p.72, 92 and 96, to Laurie Sparham for the photograph on p. 13 and to Dave Hinder and the University of Reading for the photographs on pages 26, 28, 41 and 83.

Viv Edwards
Jagiro Goodwin
Angela Wellings

Introduction

Jagiro Goodwin and Angela Wellings

Our aim

The central aim of this book is to make English in the National Curriculum accessible and relevant to all pupils. In attempting to meet this aim, we set out to bring together a theoretical basis for the main English profile components and practical suggestions for good practice for all schools.

Education for all?

The failure of British society and British schools to provide equality of opportunity for particular groups of individuals has been well documented (see, for example, Willey 1984). Our specific interest in relation to the English National Curriculum is the language needs of Black pupils – and here we use Black in the political sense to mean pupils of Asian, African and Caribbean origin. These needs have been much researched and debated but rarely adequately addressed in our schools.

In the last thirty years three distinct ideological stances have underpinned the education system's response to the perceived needs of Black pupils (Brandt 1986). In the late 1950s and 1960s the main thrust of schools and teachers was to assimilate and integrate Black children into mainstream British society. No modifications were deemed to be necessary to the traditional ethnocentric curriculum. Any changes were expected to come from the new arrivals rather than from the indigenous population.

If you were a speaker of a language or dialect other than English in a British school during this period, the chance that your teachers did not view this as a handicap was remote. The home language, particularly if it originated from the colonial or ex-colonial world, was considered by the majority of the teaching profession as a considerable barrier to the learning of English and 'successful integration' into the education system and the wider society. Beginners in the language were 'remediated' with intensive courses in English, either in isolation, or in withdrawal units removed from the mainstream classroom. This was overseen by well-intentioned teachers for the supposed good of the child.

Sadly and unwittingly, the parents of such children, anxious for their offspring to succeed, colluded with the prevailing assimilationist ideology. Teachers and parents remained oblivious to the immense education, social and emotional damage inflicted upon their children by a policy which sought to eradicate all traces of the home language and culture.

Attitudes to towards working class language and culture were similarly dismissive (Edwards 1983). Any departure from standard English was explained in terms of 'restricted code' which in turn, was the product of child-rearing practices which fell far short of middle class norms and expectations. The tendency of teachers was all too often to blame the victim, to place responsibility on the families of children who were failing in the education system rather than to try to identify those aspects of the system which were failing to address children's needs.

There was however, a discernible change in attitude to both linguistic and cultural diversity in the mid – 1970s when the assimilationist approach started to give way to a philosophy of multiculturalism. From the publication of the Bullock Report, A *Language for Life,* in 1975 to the Swann Report, *Education for All,* ten years later, there was a marked move towards recognising the strengths and intrinsic worth of minority languages and cultures and teachers were urged to celebrate diversity in every area of the curriculum. This multicultural approach was greatly strengthened by the increasing weight of evidence of the social, cognitive and intellectual benefits of bilingualism.

There was, however, from the early 1980s onwards, increasing pressure from Black parents who were dissatisfied with the education offered to their children. Increasingly, Black communities were identifying issues relating to the underachievement of their children which the education system had failed or refused to recognise. There were vigorous attacks on the cosmetic value of multiculturalism and its unwillingness to address the root causes of underperformance (cf. Stone 1981). The over-representation of Black pupils in special education units in certain education authorities confirmed their knowledge that the education system had failed their children. A handful of LEAs responded to the pressure with anti-racist education policies which set out to address inequalities and discrimination within the system.

The National Curriculum

What then of the philosophy and ideology behind the National Curriculum? Many critics have described it as 'colour blind' since it does not take as its starting point the multilingual and multi-faith nature of British society. From that standpoint, it could be argued that the National Curriculum and the Education Reform Act which provides its framework, is informed by an assimilationist ideology (Davies et al. 1990). In thirty years it would seem that education has come full circle particularly in its response to Black pupils.

The position taken in this book however is that, within the framework offered by the National Curriculum, there are many opportunities for extending and promoting good practice for all within the context of education for racial equality.

Whole school policies

One of the achievements of the National Curriculum has been to focus teacher attention on the 'grand plan' and to encourage them to work together in defining and addressing common goals. Inconsistencies in approach between teachers and departments are confusing for children and frustrating for any teacher who welcomes the opportunity to discuss and deepen their understanding of the issues. The development of whole school policies on all aspects of the curriculum and related issues is critical to the quality of education offered to our pupils. We stress the importance of whole school policies on, for example, language across the curriculum (cf. Corson 1990), record keeping and assessment (cf. SEAC 1990) and education for equality (cf. CRE 1988).

A school policy must be the result of collaborative effort. It is counterproductive to give one teacher the brief to produce a statement without extensive consultation and discussion with all colleagues. Policies of this kind will fill folders gathering dust on shelves in staffrooms but fail to influence practice. Exploration and debate around an issue is ultimately more important for what happens in the classroom than the document which summarises this process.

By the same token, a school policy can never be a definitive statement of practice. We learn from experience and exposure to others who approach the same question in a different way. Any policy needs provision for monitoring and evaluation, with the expectation that there will be regular reviews.

Policies formulated by other schools can serve as a useful starting point for discussion, but can never be taken on board as they stand. No two schools are alike. The experience, attitudes and backgrounds of individual teachers will vary enormously, as will the school population and existing practice. One aim of this book is to help readers identify the areas and concerns which individual teachers and whole staffs need to address in developing whole language policies if they are serious in their intent to provide equal opportunities for all pupils.

The structure of the book

The book falls into two main sections. In the first section, the main profile components of the English curriculum – oracy, reading and writing are examined, together with media education, an area of study which is receiving recognition for the first time in the National Curriculum English document. We look at ways of ensuring that the content and delivery of English in the National Curriculum is responsive to the needs of all children and make specific suggestions to ensure that the methodology and activities are outlined within the framework of education for racial equality.

In the first three chapters, Viv Edwards and Angela Redfern discuss current theories on how children acquire the basic skills of speaking, listening, reading and writing. They provide inspiring ideas for teachers on good classroom organisation and the kinds of activities which promote oracy and literacy skills. Each of these chapters stresses the benefits to be gained for all by the presence of bilingual and bidialectal pupils, whose linguistic expertise is a precious classroom resource.

The specific language skills which can be developed in the exploration of the media are examined by Elizabeth Pye in chapter four. Elizabeth defines 'media literacy' and raises the important issue of detecting bias. As in the previous chapters, there is a wealth of practical ideas for classroom activities.

The division into oracy, reading, writing and media education implies a compartmentalisation which bears little relationship to the reality of classrooms.

We are dealing with inter-related language skills which constantly reinforce each other. Most language related work will involve listening and talking, reading and writing and critically engaging in the task in hand. In the second part of the book, therefore, we present three case studies which describe a range of projects which have taken place in different schools. These projects fulfil the requirements of the National Curriculum in creative and challenging ways. They draw upon the diverse backgrounds of the pupils and offer the teacher practical suggestions for extension and follow-up activities, thus translating theory into practice.

In chapter five Jagiro Goodwin and Angela Wellings describe a project in an urban primary school where the pupils were actively engaged in the critical task of evaluating books in their library. The case study outlines how children can accurately detect racial bias, omission and stereotyping in texts.

Saroj Mistry describes in chapter six how she used a story as a vehicle for raising fundamental human rights issues, while enabling the pupils to develop particular linguistic skills.

The final chapter concentrates on a national arts initiative, in which Sheena Vick describes the projects she coordinated in two very different schools. These case studies highlight the exciting and varied extension work which can be done in the areas of oracy and literacy as a result of working with Black artists in schools.

The pages which follow should be seen as a contribution to the debate on good English teaching and a constructive response to the challenges of the National Curriculum, rather than a marginal issue of interest only to working in inner city schools.

References

Brandt, G.L. (1986) *The Realization of Anti-Racist Teaching.* London: Falmer Press.

Bullock, Sir A. (1975) *A Language for Life.* London: HMSO.

Commission for Racial Equality (CRE) (1988) *Learning in Terror.* London: HMSO.

Corson, D. (1990) *Language Policy Across the Curriculum.* Clevedon, Avon: Multilingual Matters.

Davies A., Hollond J., Minhas R. (1990) *Equal Opportunities in the New Era.* London: Tufnell Press.

Edwards, V. (1983) *Language in Multilingual Classrooms.* London: Batsford.

School Examinations and Assessment Council (SEAC) (1990) *Records of Achievement in Primary Schools.* London: HMSO.

Stone, M. (1981) *The Education of the Black Child in Britain.* London: Fontana.

Swann, Lord (1985) *Education for All.* London: HMSO.

Willey, R. (1984) *Race, Equality and Schools.* London: Methuen.

Part One

The Curriculum

CHAPTER 1

ORACY

Angela Redfern and Viv Edwards

Teachers need to organize the learning in ways which follow on logically and consistently from the successful language learning which children have already accomplished in the context of their own homes.

The Cox Report (DES1989)

In discussing children's language, the logical place to start is with listening and speaking, or oracy skills. As we develop, other language skills, such as reading and writing, interact with and mutually support our performance in listening and speaking. But, chronologically at least, oracy precedes literacy. We start, then, with an account of what we know about listening and speaking. We look both at those aspects of oracy which apply to all children, irrespective of their language background, and also at those aspects which are particularly important for bilingual and bidialectal speakers.

Interestingly, far less attention has been given by teachers and educationalists to oracy than to other aspects of language development. It is only recently that research on the learning process has thrown light on the importance of talk. Innovations in classroom organisation and practice which reflect this new understanding were not necessarily developed with bilingual children in mind. It is significant, however, that good practice in oracy, as in other areas of the language curriculum, is beneficial for *all* children, but is especially beneficial for children in the process of learning another language.

In this chapter we will look at:

- what we know about children learning to talk
- oracy across the curriculum
- classroom organization
- the importance of providing a good role model
- how to promote positive attitudes towards talk
- what kinds of support the teacher can offer
- activities which promote oracy, including story, word play and drama
- record keeping and assessment
- resources for oracy

In looking at oracy in the classroom, special emphasis will be laid on opportunities for using other languages and dialects. This approach has obvious advantages for bilingual and dialect-speaking children: it acknowledges that linguistic diversity is a rich resource and enhances their status in the eyes of their peers. But it is also valuable for monolingual pupils. As the Kingman Report (1988) on the teaching of English points out 'knowledge about language' is essential for broadening the perspectives of all children.

What we know about children learning to talk

Our understanding of the process of language acquisition in children has gone through various quite distinct stages in the last thirty or so years. The behaviourist position was that language, like all behaviours, is learned. The adult's role was seen as selectively reinforcing skills and the child was considered to be a passive recipient. Nativists moved the emphasis from environmental influences to an innate Language Acquisition Device (LAD) which, on receipt of input, would generate grammatical sentences. The child was seen as if in a social vacuum and, once again, was credited with no active role to play. Subsequently, there was a move from the preoccupation with phonology and grammar to the development of a functional or interactional model, where the focus lay on children 'learning how to mean'.

The findings of the Bristol Language Project (Wells 1987), a longitudinal research project carried out throughout the 1970s and beyond, have been particularly influential. They demonstrated that language development is not merely a question of learning the phonological and grammatical features of a language but is rather a question of making sense of the world in the social situations of everyday life. A child acquires language by talking and listening in meaningful contexts, by using language as a means to an end. In such purposeful interactions, knowledge about language grows and expertise in using language to gain control over the world increases. Children ask questions, initiate conversations, play an active part in their own learning. It is by responding, encouraging, supporting, participating and *not* by direct instruction that adults facilitate this process.

By the age of 5, the majority of children have a large vocabulary and have gained control over the sound system and the main structures of their language. By this stage, they have become adept conversationalists, able to initiate, respond, ask, answer, take turns, monitor, gain and hold attention, channel, manipulate. Yet there is still a role for the school to play. By interacting with interested adults and by absorbing language from books, heard or read, children's vocabulary continues to grow, more complex structures will become part of their linguistic repertoire, more subtle and precise uses of language, such as puns and metaphors, will be learned. Language development is a lifelong experience.

Traditionally, British society has not greatly valued children's talk: 'Children should be seen and not heard' or 'Speak when you are spoken to' are expressions that many adults today will have heard as children. 'Sh! Sh!' 'Be quiet and get on with your work!' are familiar refrains from our own schooldays and we have listened with awe to grandparents' tales of canes and straps being administered for the crime of daring to talk in class. Although there have been significant steps forward in attitudes towards talk, there is still a great deal of work to be done to dispel the myth that talking in school is synonymous with idle chatter, or wasting time. The English National Curriculum document provides us with much needed backing. For the first time, 'speaking and listening' have been accorded equal status with 'reading and writing,' a powerful force for convincing colleagues, parents and children that oracy should be taken seriously. The work of the National Oracy Project is also doing a great deal to promote the status of talk and listening in education.

There are many sound educational reasons for promoting oracy. We now know that talk is a vital instrument in the learning process on several different fronts. Firstly, there is the social aspect of talk (since learning does not take place in a vacuum) which allows us both to communicate and to build relationships. Secondly, there is the cognitive aspect which develops understanding through hearing, digesting, responding and experimenting *through talk*. And thirdly, there is the linguistic aspect whereby, through talking, the child's knowledge about and control of language develops.

In a world transformed by information technology, the role of the teacher has changed dramatically. Teachers can no longer be seen as the fount of all knowledge, feeding children facts to be learned by heart. We have made a great deal of progress from the traditional model where teachers monopolized classroom talk and asked all the questions. There is a growing awareness, too, of the pseudo-nature of the questions that are a feature of many classrooms, where teachers already know the answers and children are required to provide a particular response. We know that children learn most effectively by engaging in purposeful and meaningful activities – real debate, genuine dialogue and inquiry, decision-making, problem-solving. This is how they make new knowledge their own.

Oracy across the curriculum

It is possible to promote oracy in the classroom in many different ways. An essential first step is the realisation that oracy skills can be encouraged not simply as part of the work in English but as an integral element in work across the curriculum. It is also important to think about aspects of classroom organization and their effectiveness in encouraging meaningful talk. Teachers have a responsibility, too, for examining their own attitudes towards talk, particularly the language repertoire of dialect-speaking and bilingual children, and considering ways in which they can promote linguistic diversity as a classroom resource. Oracy in all its many forms, must be presented as something positive: teachers need to provide a thoughtful role model for their children and also to develop strategies to support less confident members of the class.

It may seem a mammoth task to fit talk into the timetable with all the various other demands of the National Curriculum. History, Geography, Technology, etc. are all jostling for their bite of the educational cherry. For once there is an easy answer: it is not a question of *more,* but of *different*. Talk is a mode of learning in all subject areas, across the whole curriculum. By shifting the emphasis from working in isolation, pen in hand, to working in a genuinely collaborative way, talk can come into its own in a wide variety of ways:

- brainstorming
- describing events
- presenting an argument
- recalling events
- expressing opinions
- interviewing
- carrying out surveys
- talking to visitors

- planning work
- reflecting on finished work
- reporting findings
- explaining a case
- justifying a position
- commenting on others' views
- using the telephone
- giving and following instructions

Classroom organization

Classroom organization is a question which has to be considered very carefully. Rows of desks are well-suited to a 'chalk and talk' approach to teaching but do nothing to foster the kind of collaborative learning through talk which we need to promote. The kinds of issues which should be addressed include the following:

- arranging the furniture to allow a variety of contexts, e.g. pairs, small groups, larger groups, etc.
- allowing for a large area where the whole class can gather for discussion and to share experiences
- remembering the proven value of the circle as a means of facilitating talk
- arranging for private areas where children can talk in confidence
- encouraging variations on the Home Corner, such as the space station, the bicycle shop, the hairdressing salon, for Key Stage 2 children whose role-play needs are often ignored.
- ensuring easy access to materials and establishing classroom ground rules from the start. This minimises the amount of teacher time wasted on management and organisational matters.
- being aware that the composition as well as the size of the group will affect children's oral language performance - and that the teacher needs to be aware of the effect which sex, race, culture, age and ability will have on the talk, as, too, will factors such as whether the group is teacher-imposed, child-selected, with or without teacher, etc.

Role models for talk

Teachers wishing to promote learning through talk in their classrooms also need to think very carefully about their own behaviour and the kind of model which they offer in their interactions both with children and with other adults. It is clearly important to:

- offer a good model of a listener - listen attentively and respond warmly to children's comments
- be a genuine participant in discussions rather than a supervisor or a judge. Show trust in the children by sharing personal stories from your own family life

- avoid repeating what children say – leave the power with them and they will soon learn to be audible
- encourage an atmosphere of cooperation and collaboration rather than competition, if successful group work is to thrive
- remember that interactions between adult members of the school community will give hidden messages to children about respect for individuals
- share your feelings and emotions as well as factual anecdotes with children and encourage children to express their emotions openly without fear of being ridiculed
- be prepared to discuss sensitive subjects openly, e.g. bullying, racist name-calling. (Practical advice on responding to difficult questions such as this is given in publications listed under *Racism* in the resources section at the end of this chapter)

Positive attitudes to talk

Oracy, then, has a central role to play in the educational process. It is important to remember, however, that language is not only an essential element in the development of thought or the communication of information. It is an integral part of who and what we are, what we feel and what we think. It also acts as a trigger for powerful social, gender and racial stereotypes and as a means of perpetuating existing social inequalities.

There is no shortage of research findings which support this position. The discourse strategies employed by boys ensure that, as a group, they demand and receive far more teacher time than girls. Female discourse style is far more co-operative and non-confrontational (cf. Graddol and Swann 1989). Similarly, there is evidence that teachers tend to evaluate the speech of children from different class and ethnic backgrounds quite differently (Edwards 1983). For instance, in research on working class English, middle-class English and African Caribbean children, a hierarchy of preferences emerged: middle-class children were considered to be more intelligent and competent than working class children who, in turn, were considered to be more intelligent and competent than children with recognisably Black speech.

Stereotypes abound. It is a common assumption, for instance, that only middle-class English-speaking families offer a sufficiently stimulating environment and that the school needs to compensate for the assumed linguistic deprivation of many children's homes. Recent in-depth study of the language of home and school, however, has exploded this and similar myths (Tizard and Hughes 1984). The main differences in language use occur not between middle- and working-class families but between home and school. At home, conversations are frequently longer and more equally balanced between adult and child. Children ask more questions and spend more time in conversation with adults. The notion that professionals should offer advice and suggestions on how parents should talk to their children is seriously challenged by findings of this kind.

It is crucial that teachers should be aware of differences in discourse style and guard against social and racial stereoptypes. Under no circumstances should we make value judgements about children's personality or intelligence because of the way they talk. The same teaching principles apply to oracy as to literacy. It is the teacher's responsibility to respect the language of the home and to respond to the *meaning* of a child's contribution, not its surface features. It goes without saying that teachers should:

- respond equally positively to all the dialects and languages which children bring from home so as to rule out any anxiety a child might have about 'correctness' or 'mistakes'
- remember that attitudes towards class, culture and race affect attitudes towards language and be ready to counteract negative attitudes towards non-standard English speakers and speakers of other languages

Providing support

Although the benefits of providing opportunites for learning through talk are beyond question, there are also certain pitfalls which teachers must avoid if they are to provide a supportive environment for all the children in the class:

- respect the need for confidentiality if children divulge personal stories
- avoid a 'hands-up' strategy in whole class situations – try instead a magic stone, a pretend microphone, a TV screen, etc., while children's ability to take turns becomes established
- watch for domination of a group by one individual – pairwork leading to foursomes is more likely to ensure a balanced distribution of power
- if group work is new to the class, be ready for some disharmony at first – encourage children to set their own rules and support them in seeking solutions to their difficulties
- be honest and let the children know that consensus is not always possible but that everyone must be allowed the opportunity to put their point of view
- don't try to make children address the whole class too soon – this can be a daunting experience

The sensibilities of all children need to be taken into account when planning activities which promote oracy. The specific needs of bilingual children, however, deserve particular attention. When children from the New Commonwealth who spoke no English arrived in British schools in the 1960s and 1970s, the early response was to withdraw them to special 'language centres' where they received intensive instruction in, and through, English until they reached the point where they were deemed to be able to manage in a 'normal' classroom. The home language was largely overlooked and the main task of the teacher was to assimilate children as quickly as possible into the mainstream.

There was, however, increasing dissatisfaction with provision of this kind. Many people began to realise that 'withdrawal' – either to a special centre or to a special class within the school – did not offer the optimal language learning environment. There was little or no access to English-speaking peers who could offer the best models for natural language use; opportunities for using English were often contrived rather than spontaneous; and, equally damaging, children who were withdrawn for language teaching were inevitably denied access to the full range of curriculum activities on offer to English-speaking children.

The focus therefore moved to supporting emergent bilingual children in the classroom. Sometimes this has taken the form of a language support teacher working collaboratively with the classroom teacher, advising on the content and delivery of lessons. More recently, bilingual support teachers have also begun to work in schools, helping children by consolidating the language skills that children bring with them from home and also by explaining things, where necessary, in the home language.

Many inner city schools are used to dealing with children who arrive with little or no English. By working co-operatively with language and bilingual support teachers, many mainstream staff have acquired a wide range of skills and a good understanding of the needs of emergent bilinguals. In many other schools, however, non-English speaking children arrive much more rarely. There will be perhaps just one or two children in the entire school and teachers will, understandably, have far fewer ideas on how best to help them. The following suggestions work well in both situations:

- make the child comfortable in an environment which is new and strange. Provide a peer support partner straightaway – another child who speaks the same language is an obvious choice, where possible; forge strong links with the home; and be especially sensitive when arranging your groups
- both teachers and pupils should ensure that they are able to say each other's name clearly and with correct pronunciation. It is also important to name languages properly, for example *Panjabi, Urdu, Gujarati* and not *Indian* or *Pakistani*
- teachers should avoid speaking slowly and in a stilted fashion. Bilingual pupils need to become familiar with correct pronunciation, intonation and rhythm and they need to hear the normal contractions of language (*don't* not *do not; I've* not *I have,* etc)
- pupils should be involved in the normal range of classroom activities
- teachers should avoid putting too much pressure on pupils to speak, particularly in the early stages. They should ensure that when a pupil is called upon to respond, a pattern of response has already been established.
- if teachers analyze the learning task and consider ways in which to present it with maximum support, the whole class will benefit. For example, provide picture cards for story-telling; use visual materials to reinforce 'key' words and concepts.

Activities which promote oracy

Teachers have a responsibility to provide activities that encourage listening and talking for a wide range of purposes, in a wide variety of styles, for many different audiences. It is helpful to remember that quality of experience counts and to ensure children's total involvement and pleasure in the activity. It is also important never to underestimate children: always make new demands and offer new challenges. The possibilities are endless, and the following suggestions are just some of the activities which can be used very effectively for promoting children's oracy skills:

Stories and storying

'We perceive the world narratively, handle experience by composing it into stories.'

Harold Rosen

Teachers are well aware of this. Day in, day out, they witness the power of story in their classrooms. Throughout Key Stages 1, 2 and 3, a strong case can be made for reading regularly to children. Though nothing is taught explicitly in 'Storytime,' listening to stories is an amazing learning experience. Children discover:

- how to make sense of their own experiences and grow emotionally
- greater knowledge of others, including the ability to empathize
- new worlds in time, place and imagination
- a wide range of social issues
- literary and poetic vocabulary
- the needs of the audience and the concerns of the writers

But above all, listening to stories helps children to learn about ways of responding to texts: predicting, recalling events, comparing with other stories; appreciating humour, suspense, dramatic irony; articulating reasons for liking or disliking certain aspects of the story; recognizing stereotypes and bias; applauding authentic detail and dialogue. Children who respond to stories with a questioning mind from the earliest age will be less likely to be manipulated by the print and visual images which they encounter throughout life.

Reading stories is an integral part of most teachers' classroom practice. Telling stories is possibly a less-developed skill, but one well worth acquiring. There is no barrier between the storyteller and the children, contact is real and captivating. It is possible to reshape the story to suit the audience and, by skilful use of pacing, pauses, intonation, gesture and expression, children can be helped to create images in their minds. Story patterns with rhyme, rhythm and repetition encourage listeners to become involved in the telling and join in the refrains. Cumulative and repetitive stories also help the audience anticipate the next incident and the final outcome. The immediacy of story-telling makes this an activity which all children enjoy, but the extra visual and structural supports are particularly helpful for second language learners.

Anyone unconvinced of the value of story-telling need only witness a performance by one of the many professional story-tellers who work with children in schools. While few of us can aspire to such a stock of stories or so polished a delivery, we all have the potential for story-telling. A useful starting point is to tell stories from your own experience which will trigger memories in children and encourage them to do the same. Children, of course, are often at the centre of their own storying, which puts them on a par with better-known heroes and heroines and can be most affirming. Folk tales from around the world also offer a rich source for sharing: they deal with great emotions and universal truths, and are filled with images that create a powerful atmosphere.

By drawing on your own experience, if you speak another dialect or language, or by involving parents and colleagues from different language backgrounds, it is possible to include a wide range of dialects and accents in story-telling. This can be achieved in many different ways:

- the teller can provide a brief synopsis before starting the story
- the teller can intersperse the use of the other language or dialect with English commentary
- if the teller speaks no English, a second party – maybe a child – can act as interpreter
- children can be provided with key words and asked to spot them or join in with refrains as the story proceeds

In the same way that children learning English find story-telling a valuable and exciting experience, English-speaking children can be captivated by hearing stories in other languages and dialects. It is also helpful to create a bank of stories in a range of languages, dialects and accents which can be enjoyed by bilingual and bidialectal children and allow monolingual speakers to experience the different sounds and rhythms.

Savouring language

Children in particular are fascinated by word games - by puns, backslang, tongue-twisters, conundrums, double meanings, anagrams, palindromes, etymologies and 'secret' languages.

The Kingman Report (DES 1988)

Part of the teachers' role is to encourage children to savour language, to develop an ear for its sounds, rhythms and nuances. Experience accumulated by listening to and experimenting with language is never wasted. It forms a stockpile on which children can draw in their own stories and storying. There are many opportunities for enjoying the music of words and the patterns of language in:

- games such as I spy, I went to market, The minister's cat, etc
- jokes, riddles and limmericks
- alliterative poems, onomatopoeia, new words for old songs
- listening to and creating poems on tape in a wide range of dialects and languages
- class topics on language – surveys of language use in school; Cockney rhyming slang; slang expressions; derivations of words and archaic expressions; rhymes, lullabies and playground games from different parts of the country and different parts of the world
- oral culture, traditional and contemporary - work on riddles and proverbs, ritual insult, story-telling, chants, vocal jazz and call and response; use the strong rhythmical beat of rap to reinforce key concepts in science or other areas of the curriculum

Particles Rap

Particles! Molecules! Atoms!
Particles! Molecules! Atoms!
My name's Atom, I'm the smallest of the bunch
I was on my own till I met up with this bunch
I was living on my own and dying for a friend
So I met up with this one, now she drives me round the bend

My names Molic - short for molecule
I'm in the middle of this bunch and boy, what a crunch!
I met up with an atom in a glass of gin
And we dribbled down the chin
So she wiped it off onto her hand
And then we ..... evaporated
        evaporated!

Now it's my turn, it's time to burn
You'll find me in alcohol, it don't come cheap!
You've gotta watch this bottle, it's got a leak.
So this just might give you a clue
To what particles really are – they're in loads of things near and far
Particles! Molecules! Atoms!
Particles! Molecules! Atoms!

Year 8 pupil, Wootton Bassett School Wiltshire, quoted in *Talk* 2: 39

Drama

> Drama deals with fundamental questions of language, interpretation and meaning
>
> The Cox Report (DES 1989)

Drama is important because it is a subject in its own right: it is a method and a learning tool. It enables children to:

- gain a better understanding of themselves and others
- gain confidence in themselves as decision-makers and problem-solvers
- explore the whole spectrum of social situations and moral dilemmas
- challenge assumptions
- explore the whole range of human feelings, positive and negative, in a safe environment
- accept rules
- organize and order events
- work collaboratively
- develop listening skills
- make sense of symbols
- extend their language repertoire
- develop non-verbal language skills such as eye contact, facial expression, gesture, movement, mime

Games and drama

Co-operative games, such as Knee-Touching, Sticky Toffee and Trains, can be a useful, non-threatening step in introducing children to the basic Drama principles. They provide opportunities for the teacher to get to know the children, and for the children to get used to being in a large, empty space and working to a set of rules.

Games can also be developed into narrative by the teacher asking questions and offering alternatives. For instance, 'Grandmother's footsteps' could be played in the normal way at first and then extended:

- who is Grandmother?
- who are the others?
- is it happening today or in the past?
- is it here or somewhere else?
- are the people rich or poor?
- are they on the right side of the law or not?

Thus, while encouraging the children to have power over the actual narrative, the teacher is able to manipulate the context for learning (for example whole groups, small groups, pairs) and the strategies (for example, 'freeze' techniques and 'photostills,' which allow children to reflect on decisions; whether to go into role to move the Drama forward).

Stories and drama

As long as the content is appropriate, stories of all sorts – traditional or contemporary, familiar or new – can serve as a springboard for Drama. An unfamiliar story, invented for the occasion might take the following form:

- the place: one side of a mountain
- the people: the villagers who live there
- the situation: one of the villagers is seriously ill
- the problem: the flower necessary for the cure grows only on the other side of the mountain

Although the teacher provides the framework, the children will have to make choices, negotiate and solve problems. For instance, who precisely will cross the mountain to get the flower? What plans will need to be made for the journey? What do they need to take? How will they tackle unforeseen problems en route? How will they communicate with the people on the other side of the mountain?

The use of Drama to explore this theme might have many different motivations. The teacher may want to introduce co-operative work in a class unused to operating in this way. But the Drama might also grow out of a class topic on travel, a shared book about illness or the need for children to do map work. It might also grow out of a desire to explore language diversity (communities on the two sides of the mountain may speak different languages) or to explore acceptance and tolerance.

The quest for the flower is an example of a tale invented for the occasion. Familiar stories can be used to similar effect. Children often reconstruct stories they have enjoyed in their own role play, but Drama offers possibilities much wider than mere reconstruction. A Nativity play, for instance, can be transformed by asking questions:

- are the children participants in the original story – the Shepherds or the Wise Men? Or are they onlookers – historians, journalists or archaeologists?
- what special problem will the children try to solve? For instance, the shepherds might need to find lost sheep or deal with marauding wolves; archaeologists might find clues which carry the investigation further

Bilingual drama

Drama is an ideal activity for encouraging the appropriate use of different languages, dialects and accents. Many families switch between different languages or dialects, depending on the situation, the subject and who they are talking to. It is only natural that this pattern should be reflected in drama dealing with domestic situations. Similarly there are many occasions when speakers of one language come into contact with speakers of another and need to develop strategies for communication. Bilingual drama provides opportunities for bilingual children to develop their skills as interpreters as they explain to other members of the group what has been said. It also helps develop the language awareness of monolingual children.

Visiting groups

In addition to developing Drama as a normal part of classroom activities, teachers may also want to make use of visiting groups such as 'Theatre in Education' which visit schools to explore a particular theme, usually a moral issue, such as the rights of minorities. When theatre groups work in school for only a day, however, there is a danger that the complex issues which are being explored will be oversimplified. For this reason, teachers are expected to do preparatory and follow-up work around the theme.

Record keeping and assessment

Oracy is a new area for assessment and many teachers are concerned about their own lack of experience. It is important to remember, however, that the aim of assessment should be to allow teachers to plan future activities to improve children's learning opportunities and to ensure further development. The aim should *not* be to label children. It is also worth remembering that the national requirement is for attainment levels to be assigned only every few years, towards the end of a key stage. At this point, teachers within and between schools can meet to moderate interpretations and to ensure a common standard.

It is helpful at this point to distinguish between National Curriculum Attainment Targets and programmes of study. The Attainment Targets are extremely narrow, offering a much more limited focus than is suggested in the programmes of study and non-statutory guidelines. This is especially true of the English Attainment Targets which are process-orientated and not content-orientated as they are, for instance, in Maths or Science. Our main concern must therefore be to deliver the programmes of study rather than to teach to the attainment targets.

To describe children's achievements and progress in the kind of detail which teachers need for monitoring and planning purposes, we have to move beyond the grids and checklists of attainment levels to a more open format of assessment. The longitudinal system of assessment already in place in some schools has much to recommend it. On-going formative and diagnostic records feed into a summative assessment, perhaps yearly when children move on to another teacher. (See *The Primary Language Record* (Barrs et al. 1988) as an example of this kind of record of achievement).

Assessment and linguistic diversity

Because of the tendency to label departures from the standard as evidence of a language deficit, teachers often respond very negatively. Take the case of Monsoor, an Urdu-speaking child who has been in England for less than a year and who uses forms like 'We cut wood and bring home' or 'We like to go swim.' This child may be deemed to have 'language problems' which need to be remedied. It is more helpful, however, to focus on other questions. How long has he been in England? Does he manage to communicate meanings successfully?

B

Monsoor has been in England for nine months now. His spoken language has developed tremendously in this time. After an initial 'silent period', he has grown in confidence and now communicates meanings very successfully. He clearly enjoys group work and makes active contributions to discussion. Sometimes he gets very frustrated when he does not know a word. I have made sure that he works in a group with another Urdu speaker who can act as interpreter when necessary. Sultan has been a great support in recent months.

A number of points need to be taken into special consideration in assessing the oracy skills of children who speak languages or dialects other than standard English:

- be aware of the social, gender and racial stereotypes associated with language and ensure that your assessments of children's language are not influenced by these stereotypes
- despite the fact that the National Curriculum Council retained the title 'English' rather than 'Language', it is essential, for reasons already outlined, to foster and record bilingual children's progress in all their languages
- always take into account the length of time a child has had contact with English, regardless of chronological age
- amount of talk is not necessarily significant. A few opportune words can move a group's thinking forward very effectively
- silence does not always mean a lack of understanding. Receptive language is always in advance of productive language

Gathering evidence for oral assessment

The following people need to be involved in assessment of oracy, as indeed of other language skills:

parents. Involve a child's parents at the beginning and end of the year in a conference to establish a complete picture of the child as an oral language user. Be prepared to have a fluent home language speaker present, if needed, both for personal support and to act as an interpreter. Areas to be covered might include, for example, how many languages or dialects do they speak? With whom?

Interest in TV, radio, cinema, videos, concerts, records? Favourite topics of conversation? Special interests? Attendance at religious or community school? Any concerns? Remember that if the school has not established beyond doubt its commitment to cultural and linguistic diversity, parents' reactions to questions about language use may be suspicious or evasive.

children. Since taking responsibility for your own learning is a powerful ingredient for progress, involve the children in the assessment – who do they enjoy talking to? In which language? Who do they prefer working with and why? What do they see as their strengths as a talker? What are their concerns? Again, in the case of dialect speaking and bilingual children, reactions will only be direct and honest if the school has successfully communicated its commitment to linguistic diversity.

all adults who have contact with the child in school: headteacher, bilingual support teacher, language support teacher, classroom assistants; be sure to consult community language teachers in the case of those bilingual children who attend classes.

Informal observation

Teachers are excellent observers. During normal classroom activities, while interacting with your children, you will pick up a mine of information which can be noted in the child's formative record. This need not be a mammoth task – one observation can cover several purposes and the comment need only be brief, pointing out any significant change in children's oracy development. Over a period you can accumulate comments in a variety of social and learning contexts so as to have a complete picture of a child's language proficiency.

Targeted/planned observations

Use this means if you or a parent or a colleague have any concerns about a particular child's language, or if you realise, on consulting your records, that there are gaps in your knowledge about a particular child in a particular context and need more specific evidence.

References

Barrs, Myra et al. (1988) *The Primary Language Record: A Handbook for Teachers*. London: ILEA Centre for Language in Primary Education.

Department of Education and Science (DES)(1988) *Report of the Committee of Inquiry into the Teaching of English* . (The Kingman Report). London: HMSO.

Department of Education and Science (DES)(1989) *English for Ages 5–16*   (The Cox Report). London: DES and Welsh Office.

Edwards, V. (1983) *Language in Multicultural Classrooms*. London: Batsford.

Graddol, D. and Swann, J. (1989) *Gender Voices*. Oxford: Blackwell.

Rosen, H. (1988) 'Stories of Stories.' Postscript to B. Rosen (1988)*And None of It Was Nonsense*. London: Mary Glasgow, pp.163-172.

Tizard, B. and Hughes, M. (1984) *Young Children Learning*. London: Fontana.

Wells, G. (1987) *The Meaning Makers*: Children Learning Language and Using Language to Learn. London: Hodder & Stoughton.

Resources for Oracy

Artists in School

Arts Education for a Multicultural Society (AEMS)(1990) *The AEMS Directory of Artists for Education*. London: AEMS.

Arts Education for a Multicultural Society (AEMS)(1990) *Resources for Arts Education in a Multicultural Society*. London: AEMS.

Afro-Caribbean Education Resource Centre (1989) *Resource and Information Guide*. 3rd edition. Afro-Caribbean Education Resource Centre, Wyvil School, Wyvil Road, London SW8 2TJ.

Dust, K. and Sharp, C. (1990) *Artists in School: A Handbook*. London: Bedford Square Press.

Dialect materials

Edwards, Viv (1990) *A Directory of English Dialect Resources: The English Counties*. From Economic and Social Research Council, Cherry Orchard East, Kembrey Park, Swindon SN2 6UQ.

Drama

Bainbridge, C. and Castillo, L. (undated) *Birbal and the Thieves*. Inter-Cultural Curriculum Support Service, Gorway Block, Gorway Road, Walsall, West Midlands WS1 3BD. [Master copies of play scene with cut out figures and scenery; ideas for use and two suggested scripts. Primary level].

Centre for World Development Education (1989) *Rafa Rafa*. CWDE, Regents College, Inner Circle, Regents Park, London NW1 4NS. [Drama simulation and role play for ages 13+ about the problems when different cultures come into contact].

Christian Aid (1983) *Drama For Justice*. Christian Aid, PO Box 100, London SE1 7RT. [Detailed suggestions for schools and youth clubs].

Gulbenkian Foundation (1982) *The Arts in School*. London: Gulbenkian Foundation .

ILEA Advisory (1977) *Drama Guidelines*. London: Heinemann.

Kops, B. and Romain, J. (1982) *In a Strange Land: A History of the Jews in Modern Times.* Michael Goulston Education Foundation, 80 East End Road, London N3 2SY. [Cassettes, pupils materials, teachers' guide].

Neelands, J. (1984) *Making Sense of Drama.* London: Heinemann.

Wagner, B.J. (1979) *Dorothy Heathcote. Drama.* London: Hutchinson.

Language acquisition

Romaine, S. (1984) *The Language of Children and Adolescents: The Acquisition of Communicative Competence.* Oxford: Blackwell.

Tizard, B. & Hughes, M. (1984) *Young Children Learning.* London: Fontana.

Wells, G. (1987) *The Meaning Makers: Children Learning Language and Using Language to Learn.* London: Hodder & Stoughton.

Oracy in the curriculum

Department of Education and Science (1990) *English National Curriculum 5–11,* London: HMSO (available from National Curriculum Council, Room 608, Newcombe House, 45 Notting Hill Gate, London W11 3JB).

Oral culture

Edwards, V. and Sienkewicz, T. (1990) *Oral Cultures Past and Present: Rappin' and Homer.* Oxford: Blackwell.

Opie, I. & Opie, P. (1977) *The Lore and Language of School Children.* London: Paladin.

Racism

All London Teachers Against Racism and Fascism (1984) *Challenging Racism.* London: ALTARF.

Commission for Racial Equality (1988) *Learning in Terror.* London: HMSO.

ILEA (1983) *The English Curriculum: Race – Materials for Discussion.* London: ILEA English Centre.

Leicestershire Centre for Multi-Cultural Education. *Racism and Resistance.* AB Printers (2D Sales), 33 Cannock Street, Leicester LE4 7HR. [Active learning materials for the secondary school for anti-racist education in drama and English].

Story

Barton, B. (1986) *Tell Me Another.* Basingstoke: Macmillan.

Bettleheim, B. (1976) *Uses of Enchantment.* London: Thames and Hudson.

Cambourne, B. (1988) *The Whole Story.* Leamington Spa; Scolastic.

Chambers, A. (1985) *Booktalk.* London: Bodley Head.

Meek, M. (1988) *How Texts Teach What Readers Learn.* Stroud: Thimble.

Protherough, R. (1983) *Developing Response to Fiction.* Milton Keynes: Open University Press.

Rosen, B. (1988) *And None of It Was Nonsense.* London: Mary Glasgow.

Theatre in education groups specializing in multicultural drama

Action Transport, 34 Elm Grove, Whitby, Ellesmere Port, South Wirral, L66 2PS.

Bac to Bac TiE Company, The Fairlop Building, Forest Road, Hainault, Ilford IG6 3HB.

Break Out, Drama Centre, Beechwood Road, Woodley, Reading.

Carib TiE, 63 Fairfields Crescent, London NW9 0PR.

The Cockpit TiE, Gateforth Street, London NW8.

Common Lore, 29 Charteris Road, London N4.

Greenwich YPT, Stage Centre, Burrage Road, Plumstead, London SE18 7JT.

Half Moon YTP, New Half Moon Theatre, 213 Mile End Road, London E1 4AA.

Keeping Mum Theatre Group, c/o Sparkbrook Centre, 31 Farm Road, Birmingham B11 1LS.

Leeds TiE, Quarry Mount School, Pennington Street, Leeds LS6 2JP.

L'Ouverture Theatre, Unit 604, Brixton Enterprise Centre, 444 Brixton Road, London SW9 8EJ.

Perspectives Theatre Co-operative, c/o Mansfield Community Arts Centre, Leeming Street, Mansfield, Nottinghamshire, NG18 1NG.

Red Ladder Theatre, New Blackpool Centre, Cobden Avenue, Lower Wortley, Leeds LS6 2JP.

Royal Court YTP, 309 Portobello Road, London W10 5TD.

Tara TiE, 356 Garratt Lane Earlsfield, London SW18.

Theatr Taliesin Wales, Channel View Centre, Jim Driscoll Way, Grangetown, Cardiff CF17NF.

Theatre Centre Ltd., Hanover School, Noel Road, London N1 8BD.

Projects

The National Oracy Project, 25 Notting Hill Gate, London W11 3JB.

CHAPTER 2

READING

Angela Redfern and Viv Edwards

Reading is much more than the decoding of black marks upon a page: it is a quest for meaning and one which requires the reader to be an active participant.

The Cox Report (DES 1989)

There can be little doubt of the importance of reading for life in Britain today. We read at home, we read at work, we read as consumers, we read for pleasure. We also read as citizens. We need to exercise our autonomy over the printed word and to evaluate critically what is put before us, whether we are dealing with a job advertisement, a newspaper report, the minutes of a meeting, a gas bill or a social security form. Literacy can be a source of power as well as pleasure.

It is therefore of very great importance that *all* children should be able to develop reading skills as efficiently and rapidly as possible. In this chapter we aim to examine:

- what we know about the reading process and the implications of this knowledge for the teaching of reading
- the influence of cultural factors on the acquisition of reading skills
- ways in which good links with the home and community can support the school in the teaching of reading
- the role of the teacher in promoting reading as an enjoyable and meaningful experience for all children
- ways in which linguistic diversity can usefully be reflected in reading materials
- the most effective ways of approaching the reading of dialect-speaking children
- the most effective ways of approaching the reading of bilingual children
- bias and stereotyping in resources for reading
- reading for learning
- recording children's reading progress
- resources for reading

What do we know about reading?

Given its central role in our lives, it is essential to provide as full an experience of literacy as possible for all children in our schools. But, before we can successfully motivate children to become discerning, enthusiastic readers, we have to be quite clear in our minds about what is involved in the reading process.

Traditionally, reading was seen as a behaviourist skill. Children were taught by 'bottom-up' methods, consisting largely of isolated drills and decontextualized exercises. They worked at acquiring a hierarchy of phonic rules and word attack skills. The reader was thought of as passive and totally dependent on the text, and word-perfect accuracy was expected. Reading materials were written in short, jerky sentences and used vocabulary graded according to syntactic and phonic difficulty. This usually resulted in contrived, stilted language which bore little relation to young readers' own usage. As one young child is reputed to have replied when asked what his book was about, 'It's not about anything – it's my reader!'

However, research undertaken since the 1960s points to a very different picture of the reading process. Traditionally, we thought in terms of readers as trapped by print, engaging in laborious word-by-word decoding. More recently, we have begun to think of readers as liberated to use *all* the strategies at their disposal, just as they did when learning to make sense of spoken language. Kenneth Goodman (1972), for instance, has shown the ways in which the 'miscues' or departures from the actual text offer a window on the reading process. We behave as active participants, bringing all our prior knowledge of the subject matter and of how language works to help us make 'intelligent contextual guesses' about the text. We then predict, select, confirm and self-correct as we seek to make sense of the print before us.

When children come to school they already have a well-developed knowledge of language. It is essential to avoid confusing them with meaningless, decontextualized exercises and to harness the meaning-making strategies which they already possess. Since meanings are exchanged in wholes and not in isolated fragments, then we must go first for wholes and gradually refine the parts later as children grow in experience.

This view of the reading process has important implications for children who speak a language in addition to English. All too often the role of reading is underestimated in the acquisition of a second language. Reading offers the same range of opportunities as speech for the learner to make hypotheses about the rules of the language and to deduce the meaning of words and idioms. But, unlike speech, there is a great deal of scope for reviewing the language input. A child may feel too embarrassed to ask a speaker to repeat a message when it is not understood, but experiences no such difficulty with reading. Some children may well find reading a more comfortable source of language than speech.

Nor should teachers underestimate the extent of bilingual children's experience in literacy in languages other than English. Many children attend classes in the evening or at weekends where they learn to read and write in the community language. There is evidence that bilingual children are able to transfer the cognitive skills associated with their first language in the acquisition of subsequent languages. Literacy skills are thus a resource to be encouraged, whether in English or in other languages.

Reading and culture

There is a great deal of evidence which suggests that cultural differences sometimes have a profound effect on children's apparent ability and motivation to read. All too often there is a mismatch between the culture of the classroom and children's culture outside the classroom. One study of the reading performance of Black American children (Labov and Robins 1972) showed that out of a sample of thirty-two Black children identified as non-members of street culture, several had a reading age which corresponded with their chronological age, and some had a reading age in advance of it. Yet out of a sample of forty-six boys who were members of street culture, just one had a reading age which corresponded to his chronological age, while the reading performance of the others was lower than you might have expected for their age. It would seem that school, in this case, had little ability to motivate children steeped in street culture.

Sometimes the desire to be seen identifying with the values of peer culture rather than with the school can be exaggerated into an elaborate charade. Cheshire (1982), for instance, recounts how a child labelled by the school as a 'remedial reader' was heard reading extracts from a James Bond novel to friends at an adventure playground. Kohl (1967) in *Thirty-Six Children* tells of similar cases in New York. In fact, many teachers will experience behaviour of this kind from time to time.

Educators respond to situations of this kind in a variety of ways. Very often they see the problem as lying with the children. They construct a pathological framework which interprets school failure as a result of the inability to speak standard English, or the lack of access to white middle-class values. This response is sometimes called 'Blaming the Victim' by those who argue that the main responsibility for educational underachievement must fall on schools which fail to respond to the legitimate needs of children from different cultural backgrounds.

Home-school links

Various attempts have been made to recognise the cultural blocks which school creates. One of the most significant developments in recent years has been the various home reading schemes in which parents are asked to hear their children read regularly. Most schemes depend on the use of report cards for comments on the child's progress and other messages which allow the teacher to monitor progress and make for good communication between home and school.

Home reading schemes were pioneered in Haringey, Belfield and Hackney and have subsequently spread to a large number of other schools in many different parts of the country. One of the interesting features of the original experiments was that they took place in urban schools which had a high proportion of working class and ethnic minority families. Support for the projects has proved to be high and has helped to put paid to the myth that only middle-class parents are interested in – and capable of – helping with their children's education. The importance of such schemes lies in the fact that they see the culture of the home as essential to children's educational development: the family is a resource, not a problem.

The message which emerges, then, is the positive effect which home involvement has not only on children's progress in reading but on their attitudes towards learning and school in general. This observation holds true even in the case of parents who are illiterate or do not speak English.

An ever-growing number of schools also draw on parental and community support for reading activities in the classroom. This is a course which is well worth pursuing, as often community expertise remains untapped simply through lack of communication, and not through lack of interest or availability. Parents and other adults can, for instance, be invited into classrooms to:

- tell their personal stories and traditional tales in English or their home language to the class or to small groups
- tape stories, rhymes and songs in a variety of languages and dialects for the listening corner
- read in their first language in parallel with the teacher in English
- participate in shared and paired reading activities with children
- work with a small group on DARTS (Directed Activities Related to Texts) activities in English or the first language (see pages 35-6)
- join the class for library sessions
- help set up a family reading group in collaboration with the school and perhaps the local library to meet monthly or half termly to discuss what everyone has been reading and enjoying

The role of the teacher of reading

Another important development in the teaching of reading is captured neatly in Frank Smith's (1984) metaphor of the 'Literacy Club.' Motivated by an enthusiastic adult all children will see themselves as readers and writers, and will therefore feel eligible and eager to join. In this environment learning should be continual and effortless, meaningful, relevant, collaborative, incidental, vicarious and free of stress.

The role of the teacher is thus to promote reading as an exciting, enjoyable and high profile activity which will appeal to all children. This can be achieved in many different ways – by ensuring an exciting range of resources and making these resources accessible to children in interesting ways; by keeping the written word in high focus; by organizing a wide range of reading activities; and by promoting reading not only for pleasure but for learning.

A rich reading diet

Taste in books varies from one person to the next and the same person may want to read one kind of book on one occasion and something quite different on the next. It is clearly important to provide a very wide range of reading materials:

- different kinds of books, fiction and non-fiction, encyclopaedias, dictionaries, thesauri
- different genres, e.g. poetry, science fiction, historical novels, adventure stories, picture books, myths, legends and folk tales
- books to cater for a wide range of interests, e.g. football, hockey, ghosts, dancing, horses
- books to cater for a range of reading levels and stamina
- books by a wide range of authors and illustrators
- stories and poems in many different languages and dialects

These materials should be easily accessible to children and displayed in interesting ways. It is possible, for instance, to whet appetites by arranging a good selection of books alongside artefacts to focus on a current class theme, or the works of a particular author or illustrator, or a particular genre.

Bilingual books

Bilingual books, or dual texts, are now available in a very wide range of languages. In most cases they draw on traditional stories in which the text is written both in English and in the minority language. Increasingly, however, there is a move towards producing dual text versions of popular children's books originally published in English. Sometimes there is also an accompanying tape-cassette. The advantages of bilingual books are two-fold. They acknowledge and show respect for a range of languages which are to be found in many city schools and therefore help support the cultural identity of ethnic minority children. They also send useful messages to monolingual English speakers: bilingualism is an asset and one which the school wishes to encourage.

It is important to point out, however, that there are certain pitfalls in the use of dual texts. The quality of translation into the minority language sometimes leaves a little to be desired. It would also be naive to assume that dual texts will necessarily have a significant impact on the development of competence in the home language, since children are likely to choose the storyline written in their dominant language. Finally, dual texts can only make strong statements about a school's respect for linguistic diversity when this same respect is reflected in all aspects of school life. If this is not the case, the use of bilingual books can be seen simply as a tokenistic gesture.

Dual texts are not, of course, the only reading materials which underline the importance of linguistic diversity in the classroom. In schools where children use languages and dialects in addition to English, the library should reflect the full range of this diversity in its stock. In addition to books, children should be able to see newspapers, magazines, comics in a variety of languages. Even when children cannot read these publications, it can be fun to guess at words or the content of a story, or to look at different scripts.

Poems, stories and songs can be recorded in a variety of languages on tape and on video and on tape-slide sets. It is also important to provide in all schools books about other languages and dialects, as well as books in translation from other languages, so that all children can access world literature.

Keeping books in high focus

> Eroll Lloyd came to our class because we wrote and told him we like his book so much.
>
> Kevin

Teachers can show their pleasure in reading-related acts in many different ways. They can:

- write to authors about their work
- invite authors, illustrators and storytellers from a wide range of cultures to run workshops in the school (see the case study on page 95)
- mount a special exhibition of the works of one 'author of the month', with posters and biographical details
- watch television programmes featuring writers and poets.
- highlight new authors and new books
- visit local book fairs and take part in National Book Week

- establish links with the local library
- run a school book shop or a book club
- timetable regular slots for sharing views about what everyone has been reading.

A wide range of reading activities

Despite the demands of other National Curriculum core and foundation subjects, literacy is at the heart of educational success and it must take pride of place. Reading activities need to be carefully integrated into the timetable and can be organized in many different ways:

- daily story time when a teacher reads to the class, allowing time for discussion. There is a strong case for reading aloud regularly to children throughout Key Stages 1, 2 and 3
- shared reading with peers
- opportunities for children to read to younger or less experienced readers
- opportunities for children to read their own writing to the class
- USSR (Uninterrupted, Sustained, Silent Reading) or ERIC (Everyone Reading In Class) when the teacher and children quietly read books of their own choice. The beginning and ending of the sessions are crucial to the quality of the experience. Children's appetites need to be whetted at the start with brief, encouraging comments about the authors and the illustrators they have chosen to read. At the end, a few minutes can be well-spent sharing children's responses to their books.

Crosswords and other word games also contribute to children's reading development by helping them to focus attention on the sound patterns of English.

Reading conferences

Reading conferences offer many valuable opportunities for addressing the needs of individual children. The aim is for the teacher and child to enjoy the book together, but reading conferences also allow the teacher to monitor the child's development as a reader. Responses to children's reading need to be considered carefully. For instance, should the miscues of dialect-speaking children and bilingual children be treated in the same way as those of their monolingual peers? The reading conference also allows teacher and child to discuss the content of a book.

The frequency of conferences depends very much on the confidence of the reader: most teachers find it helpful to arrange conferences for inexperienced readers two or three times a week, and once a week or once a fortnight for experienced readers. Inexperienced readers will need support as they read:

- first, briefly discuss the title and the cover to 'warm up' the reader, since the expectations we bring to the text will influence our ability to cope with it
- encourage children to think as they read, to predict what's coming next
- accept miscues that do not alter the meaning, e.g. *Mummy* for *mother, house* for *home*

● respond fully to the text – discuss the events in the story, the characters, the setting (for further discussion of this subject, see the section on 'Stories and Storying' in the chapter on Oracy)
● broaden the discussion to other works by the same author, similar books by other authors, what to read next and how to take the reading further, (e.g. writing a review, making a poster)

Experienced readers will be keeping their own reading record. As with inexperienced readers, discussion can focus both on the current book and other books by the same author and suggestions can be offered for future reading. Bilingual children's reading in both languages should be discussed.

> Date.
> 15ᵗʰ March.   Title   "The Village by the Sea"   Authors   Anita Desai
>
> This book is about a family in India. Their mother is very ill and their father is always goin to the toddy. I read the blurb and I liked the cover so I thought I would enjoy it. And I really did. I liked the ending best of all because their mum came back from hospital for Diwali and Hari came back from Bombay. I think Anita Desai is a good writer everyone would like her books
>
> I knew you'd love this book Shakra. I certainly did. Why don't you try another of her books " A Peacock Garden". ? I have a feeling you'll love that too – you'll need plenty of kleenex, mind you!

Reading and non-standard English

In much the same way that an inexperienced reader may substitute *Mummy* for *mother,* dialect-speaking children often replace standard English with a dialect form. There are many variations in the grammar and pronunciation of English both within the British Isles and throughout the world where English is the official language. Most of us are familiar with Cockney features like *I never done it* or *anyfink* or *bruvver* and British Black English constructions like *im see dat yesterday*. Given the weight of evidence that reading is an active process which draws on all our knowledge of the language rather than a passive exercise in decoding, it is not at all surprising that we should translate any text we are reading into our own dialect.

Teachers sometimes think that they would not be doing their job if they failed to draw children's attention to 'miscues' of this kind, but intervention is likely to be counterproductive. Constant interruptions send out the message that it is more important to read with accuracy than to read with understanding. Some children may learn to cope by reading more slowly so that they meet with fewer interruptions. Other children may choose to read in a very quiet voice which makes it difficult for the teacher to hear what has been said. Others still may simply choose to refuse to read. Repeated teacher intervention can only have the effect of detracting from the problem-solving approach to reading which we want to encourage. Providing that the meaning is not affected, it is important to respond to dialect-based miscues in the same way as to miscues made by standard English-speaking children which do not affect the meaning:

- by not interrupting the flow or 'correcting' the miscue
- by praising children when they show, through their miscues, that they are responding intelligently to the text

Reading and bilingual children

The same kinds of issue arise when we look at the reading of bilingual children. We are dealing here, of course, with a continuum of behaviour. Children who are literate in their own language but are only just beginning to learn English will have a well-developed sense of the reading process, the function of print and the use of books, but will obviously not be able to put into operation the same cue systems which are available to English speakers. Those children who speak English fluently, on the other hand, will behave in exactly the same way as native speakers, though they will also bring with them a greater insight into, and awareness of, language and cultural difference than is possible for monolingual children. Between these two poles, children's reading will reflect varying degrees of influence from the home language and progression towards control over the English sound and spelling systems, grammar, vocabulary and idiom.

In dealing with bilingual readers, the teacher therefore needs to take into account that:

- children in the process of acquiring English will make a similar range of miscues as monolingual children. They will also miss out inflectional endings and make other miscues which are indicative of their present level of competence in English. When miscues of this kind do not affect the meaning of the text, they should be welcomed as evidence that children are applying themselves intelligently to the task of making sense of what they read.
- reading gives the bilingual child the opportunity to review the text as often as is necessary and that this can be a great deal less stressful than asking

someone to repeat what they have said.
● we cannot automatically assume that because children cannot answer questions on a text, that they have not understood. It is always helpful to check this out with someone who speaks the same language as the child – a peer, a parent or another adult.
● bilingual children should be encouraged to read in their other language. Literacy activities in one language support development in the other.

Dealing with bias

'That's not right. It should be the Daddy. Mummies can't light fireworks.'

Lynda

Many books raise questions of role stereotyping based on race, gender and class. There is certainly a case for censoring certain books, especially where young children are involved. However, it is impossible to rid a collection of every book containing bias of this kind, both on economic grounds and also because the volume of literature which consciously avoids such stereotypes remains quite small. Negative content must therefore be used as a basis for discussion and for action. Together with children, it is possible to look into questions such as:

● is there adequate coverage on the subject?
● is the information up to date?
● is the author qualified to address the topic?
● is the author's stance one-sided?
● are facts and opinions confused?
● does the text perpetuate stereotypical race and gender roles?
● do visual images reinforce stereotypes?
● is there any attempt to present a complex multi-faceted society?
● are Black characters tokenistic?
● are non-Europeans presented as 'exotic'?
● are important facts left out?
● is the author attempting to manipulate the reader?

The case study on page 70 describes how teachers helped children evaluate the stock in their school library.

Reading for learning

Reading for pleasure is, of course, of central importance. But it is also important to read for information. Research has shown that children find non-narrative texts more difficult to process, yet it is critical that children develop the skills necessary for learning across the curriculum. Classroom activities which promote information retrieval include weekly library sessions which familiarize children with the cataloguing systems, help them to get to know the stock and provide experience in using an index, a glossary, a contents list, etc.

The most exciting recent development in this area, however, is the emergence of DARTS (see Lunzer and Garner 1977; 1984) which give children experience in extracting salient points in meaningful contexts for relevant purposes. DARTS fall into two main categories:

- Analysis DARTS in which the children are asked to analyze the text, for example by labelling, underlining, segmenting; then by representing the information in a different form, for example lists, tables, diagrams; and finally by using the newly acquired information, for example in designing a poster, formulating a questionnaire.

- Reconstruction DARTS, for example using cloze procedure where children are required to supply words which have been deleted; sequencing activities where arbitrarily arranged paragraphs are placed in order; or prediction activities, where paragraphs are presented one at a time and children are asked to suggest what comes next.

To support children's learning effectively, DARTS must be relevant to the class topic being studied and they must involve discussion and small group work.

Record keeping

Teachers have more experience of assessing reading than any other language skill. Standardized tests of reading are used extensively, particularly at 7 plus and on transfer to secondary school. Concern about the usefulness of standardized assessment, however, has grown over the years and testing has come under fire because:

- it throws little light on how a child sets about the task
- it often yields very little formative information which will help the teacher plan what to do next
- it tells you nothing about children's progress over time
- different tests sometimes produce startlingly different results
- standardization against a national norm disadvantages some groups, such as bilingual pupils
- the artifical test situation tends to distort true performance

There has been a move away from standardized assessment to more formative, multi-faceted approaches which seek information to guide the teacher and provide a fuller understanding of the child's reading skills.

Various people can usefully be involved in recording reading progress, including parents and the children themselves. At the start of each year, an initial meeting with parents can be very helpful in building up as clear a picture as possible of children as readers – the amount they read independently and with support in English and any other languages, their preferences and main interests. Children's own perceptions of themselves as readers should also be included. (The Primary Language Record (Barrs et al. 1988) is a good example of this kind of record of achievement).

From then on, regular reading conferences provide most of the relevant information which will be needed to monitor the children's progress. Library sessions, storytime, book sharing sessions and DARTS work will also provide

opportunities for observing the children as readers. Suggestions to bear in mind
when recording children's progress in reading include:

Attitudes

- enthusiasm for books
- evidence of widening attitudes
- level of involvement in USSR and storytime
- readiness to take part in shared reading activities
- confidence in choosing books
- favourite authors/illustrators

Reading strategies

- word for word decoder
- goes for meaning
- takes risks
- self-corrects
- uses sound-letter correspondences
- uses syntactic and semantic cues
- reading stamina
- reads out loud/ mumbles/ mouths/ internalizes

Reading to learn

- can find way round library
- uses card catalogues efficiently
- uses dictionaries and thesauri effectively
- retrieves information from maps and charts
- extracts salient points from texts

Response to books

- savours language
- responds to humour
- good grasp of how narrative works
- relates stories to own experiences
- compares across books
- reads between the lines
- discusses characters, setting and plot
- aware of author's stance
- prepared to question and discuss issues critically
- realises reading is an active, interrogative activity

References

Barrs, Myra et al. (1988) *The Primary Language Record: A Handbook for Teachers.* London: ILEA Centre for Language in Primary Education.

Cheshire, J. (1982) 'Dialect features and linguistic conflict in school.' *Educational Review* 34 (1): 53-67.

Department of Education and Science (DES) (1988) *Report of the Committee of Inquiry into the Teaching of English* (The Kingman Report). London: HMSO.

Department of Education and Science (DES)(1989) *English for Ages 5–16* (The Cox Report). London: DES and Welsh Office.

Goodman, K. (1972) 'Reading: A Psycholinguistic Guessing Game.' In N. Farnes (ed.), *Reading Purposes, Comprehension and the Use of Context,* Milton Keynes: Open University Press, pp. 78-84.

Kohl, H. (1967) *Thirty-Six Children.* New York: New American Library.

Labov, W. and Robins. C. (1972) 'A note on the relation of reading failure to per group status in urban ghettos.' In W. Labov (ed.) *Language in the Inner City,* Philadelphia: University of Pennsylvania Press, pp. 241-54.

Lunzer and Gardner (1977) *The Effective Use of Reading.* London: Heinemann.

Lunzer and Gardner (1984) *Learning From the Written Word.* Edinburgh: Oliver and Boyd.

Smith, F. (1984) *Joining the Literacy Club.* Reading: University of Reading Centre for the Teaching of Reading.

Resources on reading

Bilingual books

Roy Yates Books, 40 Woodfield Road, Rudgwick, Horsham, West Sussex RH12 3EP. Publisher and distributor of bilingual books. Catalogue available on request.

Home reading schemes

Edwards, V. and Redfern, A. (1988) *At Home in School.* London: Routledge.

Wolfendale, S. and Gregory, E. (1985) *Involving Parents in Reading: A Guide for In-Service Training,* Northampton: Reading and Language Development Centre, Nene College.

Reading guides

Contractor, C. (1987) *An Introduction to Indo-British and South Asian Literature for Teachers in Secondary Schools and Colleges.* Multi-cultural Education Centre, Bishop's Road, Bishopston, Bristol BS7 8LF.

Dabydeen, D. (1988) *A Handbook For Teaching Caribbean Literature.* London: Heinemann.

Elkin, J. (1985) *The Books for Keeps Guide to Children's Books for a Multi-cultural Society 8–12*. London: Books for Keeps.

Gunner, E. (1987) *A Handbook for Teaching African Literature*. 2nd edition. London: Heinemann.

Hughes, R. (1986) *Caribbean Literature in English - a checklist for teachers*. Mail Order Department, Commonwealth Institute, Kensington High Street, London W8 6NQ.

Oxford Development Education Centre (1986) *Books to Break Barriers. A Review guide to multicultural fiction*. Oxford Development Education Centre, 33A Canal Street, Oxford OX2 6BQ.

Scafe, S. (1989) *Teaching Black Literature*. London: Virago Education.

Stephens, J. (ed.) *ATCAL Reading Guides: African, Caribbean and Indo-British literature for the Classroom*. National Association for the Teaching of English (NATE), Birley School Annexe, Fox Lane Site, Fox Lane, Frecheville, Sheffield S12 4WY.

Warwick, R. (1979) *Indian Literature in English - a checklist for teachers*. Mail Order Department, Commonwealth Institute, Kensington High Street, London W8 6NQ.

Welch, J. (undated) *A Teacher's Guide to South Asian Literature*. Multicultural Development Service, Markhouse School, Markhouse Road, London E17 8BD.

Reading and bias

Dixon, B. (1977) *Catching Them Young*. 2 volumes. London: Pluto Press.

Klein, G. (1985) *Reading into Racism: Bias in Children's Literature and Learning Materials*. London: Routledge.

Klein, G. (1985) *The School Library for Multicultural Awareness*. Stoke-on-Trent: Trentham Books.

Reading and linguistic diversity

Wallace, C. (1986) *Learning to Read in a Multicultural Society*. Oxford: Pergamon.

The teaching of reading

Arnold, H. (1982) *Listening to Children Read*. London: Hodder & Stoughton in association with UKRA.

Beard, R. (1987) *Developing Reading 3–13*. London: Hodder & Stoughton.

Clay, M. (1979) *The Early Detection of Reading Difficulties*. London: Heinemann.

Department of Education and Science (1988) *English National Curriculum 5–11*, London: HMSO (available from National Curriculum Council, Room 608, Newcombe House, 45 Notting Hill Gate, London W11 3JB).

Goodman, K. (1986) *What's Whole About Whole Language?* Leamington Spa: Scholastic.

Hall, N. (1987) *The Emergence of Literacy.* London: Hodder and Stoughton.

Meek, M. (1982) *Learning to Read.* London: Bodley Head.

Moon, C. (ed.) (1985) *Practical Ways to Teach Reading.* London: Ward Lock Educational.

Smith, F. (1978) *Reading.* Cambridge: Cambridge University Press.

Waterland, L. (1988) *Read With Me.* 2nd edition. Stroud: Thimble.

Waterland, L. (ed.) (198) *Apprenticeship.* Stroud: Thimble.

Wray, D., Bloom, W. and Hall, N. (1989) *Literacy in Action.* London: Falmer.

CHAPTER 3

WRITING

Angela Redfern and Viv Edwards

The best writing is vigorous, committed, honest and interesting - all good classroom practice will be geared to encouraging and fostering these vital qualities.

The Cox Report (DES 1989)

Writing, like oracy, has tended to be a neglected area of the English curriculum. While a great deal of attention has been paid to the teaching of reading, our understanding of the writing process has, until recently, tended to lag behind. The present chapter will attempt to redress this imbalance, looking both at theoretical issues and at examples of good practice in the teaching of writing. Particular emphasis will be placed on responses to the writing of bilingual and dialect-speaking children and on opportunities for writing in other languages and dialects.

Among the issues we will be considering are:

- current trends in the teaching of writing
- the role and responsibilities of the teacher of writing
- the implications of linguistic diversity for writing
- the importance of knowledge about language for all children
- ways of 'publishing' children's writing
- special benefits of information technology for developing writers
- record-keeping and assessment
- resources for writing

What do we know about writing?

Traditionally it was assumed that children were not ready to learn to write until they started school, where they needed to be taught in a formal, specialized way by an expert – the teacher. It was thought necessary to provide systematic instruction, in strict sequence, of an elaborate series of rules which would enable the child to gain control over a set of skills.

Children spent a great deal of time at a desk silently copying handwriting patterns, forming letters, writing words – *practising* writing. Then they progressed to sentences and paragraphs and different kinds of punctuation. Writing, then, consisted of a daily diet of routine, repetitive, decontextualized activities, in an attempt to drill the requisite skills into the children.

As the findings of research on language in the 1960s and 1970s became more widely known, the realization grew that reading, writing, listening and talking are inter-related and that all four language modes are concerned primarily with meaning. Writing is no longer viewed as simply a question of visual perception, small motor control, hand-eye coordination. It is also a social process, influenced by cultural factors.

We live in a print-rich environment in Britain. From a very early age, children are surrounded by a variety of print forms, from bill boards to shop signs, from newspapers to greetings cards. By the time they arrive in school, most will have made that crucial intellectual leap: they will have realised that marks on paper are symbols that represent meaning.

They may also have accumulated a great deal of knowledge about the various purposes of writing, as well as about letters, figures and orientation of print on the page. Most will have handled crayons, felt tips, biros and chalk and made marks on walls, paper and steamy windows or in wet sand. Thus they will already have begun the process of becoming a writer and will be ready for an on-going dialogue with an interested, responsive adult who can act as a model and a guide until their writing reaches the standard, conventionally accepted form.

Many children in Britain today will be accomplishing this feat in more than one language with the help of adults at home, in school and in community classes. As we pointed out in the discussion of Oracy and Reading, this multilingual dimension is important for bilingual and monolingual children alike. For bilingual children, knowledge of one written language will support the acquisition of another. For monolingual children, linguistic awareness, an aspect of learning highlighted, for instance, by the Kingman Report (1988) on the teaching of English, will be enhanced by the experience of other languages in the classroom.

Key figures

Two figures, Donald Graves (1983) and Frank Smith (1982), loom large in the research on the teaching of writing. The research carried out by the first, Donald Graves, has had a major impact on what we know about the craft of writing and the factors affecting it. He aimed for children to feel part of a community of writers, rehearsing, drafting, editing and publishing their work. The rapid development of 'Writers' Workshop' activities in schools in Britain and elsewhere has grown out of Graves' research in this area.

In a similar vein, Frank Smith talks of a 'Literacy Club'. Motivated by an enthusiastic adult, all children will see themselves as readers and writers, and will therefore feel eligible and eager to join. It was also Frank Smith who focussed attention on the dual role of the writer, as composer and secretary or scribe. While secretarial skills are very necessary, there can be no doubt that composition is more crucial and must therefore take pride of place.

More recently in Britain, the work of the National Writing Project has been instrumental in ensuring that these ideas have reached a wider audience and have been translated into good practice. The National Writing Project has also begun to explore ways of introducing other languages and dialects into children's writing repertoires.

The role of the teacher of writing

The main aspects of the teacher's role in the development of writing skills are outlined below. This account is based on the findings of many writers, including Graves and Smith, and is fully endorsed by the English National Curriculum document. As was the case in the chapters on Oracy and Reading, the assumption which underlies the suggestions made throughout the pages that follow is that good practice is of benefit to *all* children, girls and boys, monolingual, bidialectal and bilingual alike.

A rich writing environment

> It was great at the Commonwealth Institute. Tamba Roy told us a story about Maroons who escaped slavery. Joma's mother covered him in oil so that the Spanish soldiers would have a problem grabbing him.
>
> Imran

> Cliff Moon visited our class. I enjoy his books. When he came to visit I got an idea that I would like to be an author.
>
> Claudine

> Bridget is a graphic designer. She showed us how she organizes things and designs layouts. I think I'd like to be a graphic designer when I grow up.
>
> Anna

Nothing is neutral in a classroom. We constantly send out hidden messages about what we value through the care we take, the time we devote, our tone of voice, our choice of words, our body language. Children must be left in no doubt as to the importance which we attach to literacy, not only as a means of enriching our personal lives, but also as a powerful tool in adult life. We can ensure that children understand this message, for instance, by:

- encouraging children to experiment with a variety of writing implements including fountain pens, roller balls, fibre tips, western and Islamic calligraphy pens and Chinese writing inks

● encouraging children to work with different colours, sizes, textures and weights of paper
● having writing in a variety of scripts and languages on display and as an integral part of classroom resources
● having a variety of dictionaries and thesauri in the classroom
● providing a message or bulletin board, a suggestion box, a post pox
● engaging in purposeful acts of writing alongside children
● setting aside a regular time to share writing
● inviting into the classroom men and women from a variety of cultural backgrounds. These could include authors, illustrators, storytellers, publishers, editors and bookbinders
● feeding children's minds through reading them literature from all over the world.

Writing for different purposes and audiences

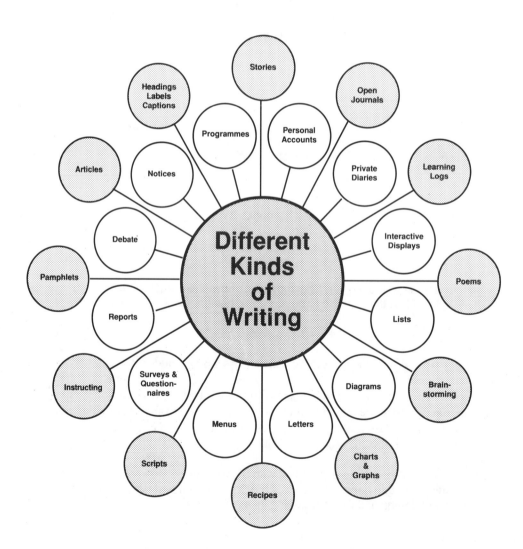

Children need support to explore different writing styles and to understand how we adapt these styles according to purpose and audience.

Functional writing is a tool which children can use to good effect both now and throughout their lives. Letters can be written to newspapers and MPs about matters of concern; posters and programmes can be designed for school events; invitations and thank you letters can be sent to special visitors.

With the growing understanding of the central role of *narrative* in all our lives as a means of making sense of the world, more time is rightly being given to children's personal storying and imaginative narratives. Experience has shown that the quality of writing is heightened when children write about people they love, about subjects that fascinate them and about powerful experiences in their lives.

It is equally important that children are given opportunities to engage in written *argument* and *debate*. The links with Media Education (see pp. 61- 8) and drama (see pp. 18-19) are obvious here. Children often have passionate opinions about matters that affect their day-to-day lives such as school uniforms, boys dominating discussions, name calling. Through watching television, reading newspapers and magazines and talking to adults, they also have views on broader issues that affect the community at large, such as 'posh' accents, cuts in Health and Education spending or South Africa.

By engaging in written argument, teasing out the pros and cons, children will gradually learn to reflect on their writing, to support their arguments with evidence, to write with greater clarity and to use persuasive vocabulary to win over their readers. This is an important area for all concerned because it affects our daily lives. It is also empowering.

Putting pen to paper

> Me and Melanie are going to do Notting Hill Carnival. I was a bit scared at first about getting lost in the crowd. But it was fantastic! You'll have to go next year.
>
> Ismene

> I'm going to tell the story of the Rani of Jhansi. I like stories where there's a woman in charge for a change.
>
> Samina

Topic choice is of crucial importance to the quality of writing, therefore it is vital that teachers listen avidly and respond to what children have to say, leaving them in no doubt as to the value of their personal storying, their feelings, attitudes and opinions. Children whose confidence has been built up in this way usually have no shortage of ideas on what they want to write about. However, if a child seems 'stuck,' it is possible to offer leads from books read, previous knowledge of the child or shared experiences. Once the topic is decided on, the next step is to help the child make choices about details of the content, by discussing, for example, the organisation of material or by airing the best starting point for the story. This 'rehearsal', before putting pen to paper, has a critical effect both on children's willingness to get started and on the quality of the end product.

Collaborative writing

If there is still some reluctance, even after preliminary discussion, to move on to the writing stage, one solution is to arrange for children to work together. Co-operating on a piece of writing is a valuable learning experience in itself, but it also provides valuable support for a child whose confidence is not yet fully established. Bilingual children can, of course, be encouraged to collaborate both in their home languages and in English.

Communal writing

Communal writing, which allows children to develop ideas, strategies and style in the security of the group, can be a great support for all writers and is particularly helpful for emergent bilingual children. By working together with an adult, children can reach a high standard of which they can feel justly proud. They can also learn a lot about the writing process and about the needs of the reader in this way.

A first step could be for the teacher to write the main points of a story or a personal anecdote, which she knows the class has previously enjoyed, on a flip chart or an OHP, encouraging the children to decide which bits to include, where to start, how to sequence the incidents, how to create different atmospheres and effects.

Pooling ideas for communal writing soon gathers momentum – retelling loved stories; extensions to well-known folk tales; accounts sparked off by school trips or visitors to the class. Most importantly, communal writing provides a good model of the craft of writing as crossings out will inevitably occur, along with changes in order, additions, omissions, searching for the most appropriate or expressive vocabulary and authentic dialogue.

Responding to children's writing

It goes without saying that we should always respond to children's writing with sensitivity and concentrate on achievements, not on errors in surface features. We can encourage developing writers by:

- receiving the work with interest and pleasure
- responding positively and in detail to the content. Writers need to know specifically what a reader appreciates and why. General comments, however complimentary, are not enough as they do not help writers to improve their technique or sharpen their critical faculties
- always writing a comment on the content. This is vital to let the writer know we are interested readers. It also provides a further model for the child

and affords an opportunity to set up an extended dialogue
between reader and writer
- avoiding, at all costs, making children feel anxious about mistakes. To make
  progress, writers must take risks
- remembering that the developmental process is the same for bilingual and
  dialect-speaking children as it is for monolingual English-speaking children.
  Therefore it is important to accept the stage the child is at, praising
  achievements and responding to the meaning of a piece of work.

Riasat

<u>News</u>

Saturday I Went to my uncle house
My uncle has new car I am going with
my uncle in to my cousins house
Saturday Zafar and his big Bredhe Whice video
Saturday I Whice WoRID of Spot
Sunday I Whice Hart to Hart

What a busy weekend you've had! Have you been in
your uncle's new car yet? It sounds very exciting.
I like watching Hart to Hart, too.

Redrafting

Not every piece of writing calls for redrafting and we need to make sure that
children are aware of this. We all have off days, for instance, when it may be
better to call a halt and start afresh on a new topic, or from a different angle, the
following morning. None the less, redrafting is central in promoting the notion of
writing as a process, as a craft. It is not, of course, about producing one rough
copy and then writing it out neatly as a fair copy. Writers can make as many drafts

as they want. And writing out a finished piece of work by hand is only one of the many 'publishing' options.

Children can be helped to redraft their writing with questions such as the following:

- Is there anything else that needs to be added?
- Is there anything irrelevant which can be left out?
- Is it suitable for the intended readership?
- Is the sequencing correct – suggest arrows or a numbering system or cutting and pasting if the material needs to be reorganized.

It is also important to support children in using language as precisely as possible, looking, for instance, for alternatives to 'went' and 'said', or for the best possible adjectives to put across their meaning. Writing style will improve, too, if children are encouraged to eliminate strings of 'ands', by introducing dependent clauses, and to recall words and phrases from books and poems read.

Editing

One day in a far away Land lived an old
Man. Nobody leked the old and he
felt sad. So one day he decided to by
a bird to talk to ☐ So he walk in
to town to be a bird. He did not have
much mony because he just spent
it on the weeks shoping when he
arrived at the pet shop ne said "pleace
could I have a bird to talk to?"

While acknowledging the importance of spelling, punctuation, handwriting and presentation in the finished product, we should not lose sight of the fact that these are only surface features which must not be allowed to interfere with the process of composition. Editing should therefore always be left until last. With inexperienced writers, a teacher will take full responsibility for editing, punctuation and spelling when the story goes for publication. Gradually, as children's confidence grows, they can be involved in collaborative editing with a teacher, other adults or a friend and, finally, will self-edit independently.

These are some suggestions for supporting children's editing:

● discuss punctuation together, jogging children's memories about capital letters, etc.
● when children are ready to self-edit, get them to read through their work after they are satisfied with the content but before they consult the teacher.
They can use symbols to indicate areas of concern, such as

$\sim$ this doesn't sound right
$\square$ punctuation query
$\bigcirc$ uncertain of spelling

Spelling

It is helpful to bear in mind the relative weightings given to composition or writing (70 per cent), spelling (20 per cent) and handwriting (10 per cent) in the National Curriculum. But while the role of composer is clearly more important, we cannot overlook the secretarial skills of the successful writer.

The traditional memorization of decontextualized spelling lists has been heavily criticized as ineffective and out of step with what we know about how children actually learn. However, various other techniques have been found useful:

● praise for good analogies in spelling errors, e.g. *broose* for *bruise*
● work on 2 or 3 spelling errors, perhaps a word frequently used or one that is almost correctly spelled
● the 'look, cover, write, check' method to reinforce the correct visual image and kinaesthetic movement. This can be repeated later in the week with a response-partner in school, or with an adult at home.
● setting aside a time to work with a small group of children on spelling patterns taken from their own writing
● other classroom activities, such as the discussion of words and rhymes or the use of word play games, dictionaries and thesauri, which continually reinforce spelling patterns

Handwriting

For most pieces of work in school, it is sufficient that it has been produced by a fast fluent hand. It is unreasonable to expect highly polished calligraphic art all the time. There are, however, many ways of laying a sound foundation for speed and legibility in younger children and for developing their aesthetic skills as they mature.

Inexperienced writers will include both younger children and older children who have recently arrived from other countries with little or no experience of formal education or of roman script. In such cases, it is important to:

- check that the penhold is comfortable. Don't be dogmatic. There is more than one way to write comfortably.
- check the height of the desk and chair for comfort
- check the position of the arm to ensure that the elbow is supported when writing
- check direction of letter formation and joins to ensure a fluid movement across the paper
- give purpose to practice - use handwriting as decorative borders when displaying work or publishing books
- remember the specific needs of left-handers. They should sit to the left of a right-handed writer, preferably with light over their left shoulder. They also need to place their paper a little further away from their body and it may help to hold the pen a little higher up.

In the case of more experienced writers, there are many opportunities for -

- encouraging calligraphy as an art
- providing a variety of calligraphic pens and inks
- fostering a real interest in aesthetic presentation
- displaying work regularly

میرا نام آمتنان یونس سے -

میں سکول جاتی ہو-

میری دو ر بہنیں ہیں -

ایک کا نام ابجم ہے اور دوسری کا نام انوار ہے -

اجم یمہ سے بڑی ہے اور انوار چھوٹی ہے -

Afshan

Writing and linguistic diversity

The teacher's responsibility is clearly to support the development of children's writing to the full. In a class which includes children who speak a variety of languages and dialects, it is important that this development is not restricted to standard English.

Bilingual writing

ایک سانپ اپنے مود میں چھپ گیا

میں آپ کو ایک کہانی بتاتی ہوں کہانی ہے سانپ کی۔ ایک سانپ ہمارے بلے کی طرف آیا اسکے بعد میرے چچا کا لڑکا ہمارے گھر آیا اور اس جگہ پر بہت سے لوگ جمع ہوگئے سانپ کو مارنے کے لیے۔ لیکن سانپ اپنے مود میں چلا گیا۔ میرے چچا کے لڑکے نے بیلچے سے سانپ کو مار دیا۔ اور وہ میری بہن سے مذاق آزمانا اور سانپ اس پر پھینکنے لگا اور وہ رونے لگی۔ میری بڑی بہن آئی اس نے میری چھوٹی بہن کو اٹھا لیا اور میں دوڑ کر گھر چلی گئی اور میں نے اپنی ماں کو بتایا میری بہن ڈر گئی۔ اس کے بعد میں آپ کو ایک اور کہانی بتاتی ہوں کہانی ہے مرغی کی اور سانپ کی۔ ایک دن میں اپنے دادا کو مرغی کانٹے میں مرغی کررہی تھی میرے دادا نے ایک سانپ دیکھا چھوٹا بلے میں چلا گیا۔ اور دوبارہ دفعہ پر چلے گئے لیکن میرا دادا ڈر گیا۔ ہم نے مرغیوں کا کانٹے دیا ہمارے گھر میں سے کوئی آدمی مرغی کھاتے نہیں سکتا اس لیے ہم اپنے دادا کو دیتے ہیں۔

ختم شد

The end

Written by Zebin   زیبن نے کھا

  The snake who hid in his hole
I am going to tell you a story
about a snake. The snake escaped from a field
on the farm my cousin came to my house and
then lots of people came to try to kill
the snake. but the snake escaped down
his hole. Then my cousin got a spade and
Killed the snake Then he tricked my little
Sister He threw the snake at her and She
cried my big sister came Then she picked
up my little sister Then I ran home and told my
mother and sisters They Were scaed.
  Now I'm going to tell you
another story about a chicken
and a snake.

Well, you know it makes you feel quite clever, really, because even the teacher can't do it and you can!

Shakra

Two main arguments can be advanced for using children's home languages in the classroom. The first concerns the role of language in defining our identity. Language is an integral part of who we are, what we feel, what we think and what we celebrate. It is a crucial component of children's views of themselves as learners and this, in turn, is the foundation stone of learning. To deny children's home languages in the classroom is to suppress an essential part of their identity. To accept the home language is to encourage self-respect in bilingual children as well as to promote respect for linguistic and cultural diversity in monolingual pupils and teachers.

But, while the home language is important both in defining the identity of bilingual children and in extending the worldview of monolinguals, it also underpins the learning of other languages. All the evidence available points to a transfer of cognitive and academic skills — including reading and writing – from one language to another. The child who has learned to write in Urdu or German does not start at square one when learning to write in English. The skills acquired during the learning of the first language are used to accelerate the learning process when a child is exposed to a second or third language. Of course, the goal remains to produce fluent written standard English, but the most effective way of achieving that end is by ensuring the development of the home language, by fostering the growth of biliteracy

Writing and dialect

Teachers always correct the way I speak and also the way I write. They mainly correct the way I write more than anything. When I write a story and I include talking I write it how I would speak. But sometimes teachers cross it out and put in how they would talk. I don't think they should do that. They should leave it as it is.

John

While the National Curriculum English document offers some latitude as regards non-standard dialects of English in speech, attitudes towards the appropriate form of language in writing tend to be a great deal more prescriptive.

Despite the arguments of sociolinguists that *all* languages and dialects are perfectly regular and rule-governed systems which fulfil the communication needs of their speakers, linguistic prejudice is very much alive and well. Labels like 'sloppy', 'lazy', 'careless' and 'ungrammatical' continue to be used about non-standard varieties of English. And the same negative attitudes which are common in relation to British dialects are also to be found in discussions of Caribbean and Black British varieties, variously described as 'broken English', 'bad English' and, even in one report from a teacher organization, as 'very relaxed like the way they walk'.

While there is a clear expectation that children should be able to write in standard English, it would be extremely short-sighted if teachers failed to develop the enormous potential for children to write both in and about their own and other people's dialects.

As the quote at the beginning of this section suggests, dialect speakers need little encouragement to write at length on their views concerning the unequal treatment of non-standard varieties of English. The potential of dialect in writing can also be explored. In plays, poetry and dialogue based on children's own lives and experiences, the use of dialect can be extremely powerful – creating a wide range of effects from sincerity to plain speaking, from spontaneity to humour. Yasmin, for instance, a twelve year-old Urdu-English bilingual, is also a fluent speaker of Lancashire dialect. She produced some impressive dialect writing, including 'Smokin' cigaretts', as part of a class project on dialect:

Smokin' cigarrets.

Ave just started wi't' cigarrets

Wen mi mam found out

She gave mi a righ' smack

Mi dad aw knooa ull abewt mi

Ell give mi a whip ar two

An mi teachers think I'm a reet smoker

Me brother will kick mi eaut of house

Cigarrets I'd kept 'abit

I smoked far ages

I geet heart disease

Mi mam warned mi, ut I took no notice

It al'turned eaut to a sticky end

Cindy Hughes' provides another example of effective dialect writing in her description of 'Work in the house.' The narrative is presented in standard English, but the dialogue switches naturally and spontaneously into the 'Patwa' which is a feature of many British Black families:

> I have two sisters and one brother, but he died. My sister has now got a little son. He is six months old. He is just getting two teeth in the front. My older sister is called Janice. We sometimes get on with each other, but we do have our ups and downs. I have got a smaller sister than me. Her name is Blondel. We have never had quarrels before.

> Me and my family are all right, but me and my mum are always quarelling because she says that I don't do enough work in the house. This is what she was saying to me: "Cindy, you don't do no frigging work in de hows, ya always guway wid ya friend dem. You na even clean de dotty stove. Since Saturday ya clean um an um na clean again."

> I said, 'So what. Yu and Alfeus always a dotty up de stove and na clean um, me and Janice always affe clean um.'

> My mother was saying, 'Alfeus na for do no work, because he a work an he bring he money gimme.'

> I just took no notice and walked off.

The teacher's task should therefore be to respond to children's writing in a positive way, extending their repertoire of styles to include, wherever possible, writing in other languages and dialects as well as in standard English. It is important to discuss linguistic diversity with children and to explore the power issues associated with different forms of language. Against this background, it is possible to discuss differences between the standard and the dialect and to introduce the notion of appropriateness. However, it is essential to show respect for children's choices. Remember that, ultimately, the child decides on whether to use a standard or a dialect form. Over a hundred years of compulsory education has demonstrated that standard English cannot be enforced!

Knowledge about Language

> I guessed them all right. If you thought hard, you could tell what it meant in ordinary English though we'd never heard the Geordie words before.
>
> Eddy

> Muslims read the Qu'ran. The Qu'ran is written in Arabic. I cannot speak in Arabic or write it but I can read in Arabic. Panjabi is the language we speak at home. Panjabi is a bit like Urdu but some words are different. I can speak a bit of Urdu but a lot of Panjabi. My Grandma and my Aunties sometimes speak in Urdu but sometimes they speak in Panjabi and I can understand that. I find Panjabi very easy, but I find Urdu as hard as anything.
>
> Safeena

The recognition of linguistic diversity as a classroom resource is clearly important for bilingual and dialect-speaking children. It legitimizes different ways of speaking; it acknowledges the very strong links between language and identity; and it enhances children's status as they find themselves in the role of 'expert'. But language awareness is important for middle class speakers of standard-English, too. It gives all children confidence in their own linguistic repertoire; it contributes to combating racism by promoting respect for other languages and cultures; and it helps them to understand how language works. As the Kingman Report (DES 1988) points out:

> Informed and socially productive attitudes will flourish in classrooms where both children and teachers are accustomed to treat language as a fit subject for study. Pupils are most likely to acquire such attitudes and accompanying attitudes through active investigation.

Teachers can help create a school ethos in which children's writing reflects a respect and growing interest in linguistic diversity by:

- respecting the expert status of children in matters relating to the languages and dialects they speak
- creating opportunities for writing about opinions on the use and status of other languages and dialects
- valuing writing in other language and dialects
- exploring possibilities for using dialect in poetry, dialogue and scripts

Publishing children's work

> When I was 'Author of the Week' everybody clapped in assembly and they all wanted to read my stories
>
> Andrea

If writing is to have a real purpose, it is vital that it should reach an audience much wider than the teacher. The possibilities are limitless. The final product can be shared with a partner, a small group or the class as a whole; older children can write for younger children; writing can be read in assembly or placed in the library for other children to borrow; it can reach a wider audience still by being published in a school magazine.

    Not every piece of writing will be suitable for 'publication' and children should be made aware that this is the case. Private journals, learning logs, personal letters and many other writing acts are clearly intended for very specific – and limited – audiences. Writing that has started to seem boring or which, even after repeated attempts, does not feel quite right, should be taken as far as children want and no further. But it is important to encourage promising pieces of writing– ones which children have enjoyed and which others will like reading – and to ensure that writing of this kind is taken through the various stages of composition and transcription until it is ready to be 'published' in a form suitable for a wider audience.

    The opportunities for 'publication' are as varied as the potential audiences – individual stories, collaborative stories, whole class stories, collections of short stories, anthologies of poems, books for younger children, joke books, song books, books of sayings, picture books, comic strips, books of recipes, puppet plays, radio scripts, alphabet books, dictionaries, guide books, information books, newspapers and magazines.

Publishing in other languages

Mi casa en Maturín

Yo me llama Lorna. Cuando yo vivia en Venezuela mi casa era bonita y Grande. En mi vivian mi abuela mi hermana, mamá y papá, en la mañana cuando yo me levantaba iua para la escuela. A las 8.00 de la mañana yo asia bastante trabajo en mi colegio, despues me iua para mi casa y me tomaba mi almuerzo y despues me ponia hacer mis tareas de la escuela.

Lorna Manzi

It is obviously important that publications should reflect the linguistic diversity of the class, the school and the wider community. There have been various successful attempts, for instance, to set up a 'community of writers' for parents and families to write their own stories in home languages which are then published and translated into English. In schools which encourage volunteer help for writing workshops with the children, parents and other community members can play an invaluable role translating children's published work from the home language into English or from English into the home language. If non roman scripts are also transliterated, monolingual children can not only enjoy the visual beauty of other writing systems, but can also attempt to read the work for themselves.

Information technology

If we're working together we do it on the computer. It's easy to rub things out.
Matthew

The computer's best – you don't actually write, you just press the buttons.
Miriam

I don't like writing because I have not got the best handwriting in the world nor the fastest, but sometimes we are made to work fast and then told off for not being neat enough.
Mary

Access to computers is an invaluable support for writers both in composition and in transcription. It is quick to alter or redraft and easy to experiment with the order of sentences or paragraphs. Spelling checkers and dictionary facilities remove anxiety about spelling mistakes and put surface features into true perspective as secretarial slips are rapidly corrected.

It can also liberate children for whom writing by hand is tiring and laborious and makes it is easier to read work back. It encourages pride in presentation with many exciting possibilities for experimentation with page lay-out, typeface and graphic design. Word processors form a useful focus for collaborative work, encouraging lots of talk and planning and pooling of ideas. They provide openings for inviting parents and community members into the classroom to work alongside children as keyboard operators. And the availability of software for non-roman founts means that it is possible, with the help of bilingual adults and older children, to produce 'professional' publications in a range of other languages.

However, one word of warning: it is an unmistakable feature of many classrooms that boys tend to monopolize the computers. Girls need to be actively encouraged to develop keyboard skills and boys should be made aware that it is unacceptable for them to take up more than their just share of time at the keyboard. This is very much an equal opportunities issue.

Record keeping and assessment

One anxiety that has developed around the National Curriculum is the fear that teaching will become assessment driven. This anxiety is very understandable. The preoccupation in the National Curriculum with assessment levels is potentially damaging because it encourages the tendency to label.

For girls, and for children who come from different social, linguistic and cultural backgrounds, assessment poses special worries. There is a long history in the UK of the educational underperformance of girls in certain areas of the curriculum and at certain levels of study. Ethnic minority and working class children also tend to underachieve: they are under-represented in selective schools, top streams and examination classes and over-represented in special education and lower streams. The cultural bias both of testing procedures and of the tests themselves has received a great deal of attention and there is now widespread agreement that bias-free tests are simply unattainable.

We need to work within the requirements of the education legislation. However, we should not lose sight of the fact that the aim of assessment is not to label children but to allow teachers to improve their teaching skills and to plan activities that will develop children's potential to the full. It is also helpful to remember that there is no need for undue preoccupation with assessment levels on a daily basis. The national requirement is for levels to be assigned *only towards the end of a key stage* when meetings within and across schools to moderate interpretations will ensure a common standard.

A particular problem arises, however, with assessments in English. Unlike other curriculum areas, the English attainment targets are not content-orientated. The checklists and grids which are becoming increasingly common in record-keeping for other areas of the curriculum are therefore very unsatisfactory in English. A much fuller and more helpful picture for teachers and pupils alike is provided by a writing profile, a longitudinal record which includes samples of children's work, covering narrative and non-narrative writing, for a range of purposes and audiences. Many schools keep ongoing formative and diagnostic records of this kind in a folder or scrapbook that feeds into a summative assessment, perhaps yearly, when most children move on to another teacher. *The Primary Language Record* (Barrs et al. 1988) is an excellent example of this kind of record of achievement.

In order to have as full a picture as possible of the children as language users, it is essential that teachers should involve in the record-keeping process the children themselves, parents and all colleagues, including community language teachers where applicable. Some suggestions to bear in mind when recording children's progress in writing include:

Attitudes to writing

- confidence as a writer
- preferences for kinds of writing (e.g. narrative or non-narrative), for subject matter and for writing purposes
- participation in communal writing activities
- preferred writing partners
- preferred writing tools
- willingness to redraft

Composition (writing)

- influence of reading diet
- desire to communicate
- awareness of audience
- organization of material
- expressive vocabulary
- use of stylistic devices, e.g. repetition
- use of tenses and pronouns
- variety of structures
- use of detail
- use of dialogue
- ability to build tension

Surface features (spelling and handwriting)

- willingness to attempt unknown spellings
- range of spelling strategies
- use of punctuation
- letter formation
- attention to layout
- aesthetic sense

It is also important to make a note of teaching strategies that have helped children in the past and to provide possible ways of moving forward.

References

Barrs, Myra et al. (1988) *The Primary Language Record: A Handbook for Teachers*. London: ILEA Centre for Language in Primary Education.

Department of Education and Science (1988) *Report of the Committee of Inquiry into the Teaching of English* (The Kingman Report). London: HMSO.

Graves, D. (1983) *Writing: Teachers and Children at Work.* London: Heinemann.

Department of Education and Science (DES)(1989) *English for Ages 5–16* (The Cox Report). London: DES and Welsh Office.

Smith, F. (1982) *Writing and the Writer.* London: Heinemann.

Resources on Writing

Gender issues

National Writing Project (1990) *What are Writers made of? Issues of gender and writing.* London: National Curriculum Council.

Handwriting

Cripps, C. & Cox, R. (1990) *Joining the ABC*. Learning Development Aids.

Jarman, C. (1979) *The Development of Handwriting Skills: A Resource Book for*

Teachers. Oxford: Basil Blackwell.

Sassoon, Rosemary (1990) *Handwriting: A New Perspective.* Cheltenham: Stanley Thorns Ltd.

Linguistic diversity

Edwards, V. (1990) *A Directory of English Dialect Resources: The English Counties.* From Economic and Social Research Council, Cherry Orchard East, Kembrey Park, Swindon SN2 6UQ.

Houlton, David (1985) *All Our Languages.* London: Edward Arnold.

National Writing Project (1990) *A Rich Resource: Writing and Language Diversity.* London: National Curriculum Council.

National Writing Project (1990) *Writing Partnerships (1): home, school and community.* London: National Curriculum Council.

Open University (1985) *Every Child's Language.* Clevedon, Avon: Multilingual Matters for the Open University.

Spelling

Peters, M. (1985) *Spelling: Caught or Taught? A New Look,* London: Routledge.

Torbe, M. (1977) *Teaching Spelling.* London: Ward Lock Educational.

The teaching of writing

Department of Education and Science (1988) *English National Curriculum 5-11,* London: HMSO (available from National Curriculum Council, Room 608, Newcombe House, 45 Notting Hill Gate, London W11 3JB).

Department of Education and Science (DES) (1988) *Report of the Committee of Inquiry into the Teaching of English.* (The Kingman Report). London:HMSO.

National Writing Project (1989) *Writing and Learning.* London: National Curriculum Council.

National Writing Project (1989) *Becoming a Writer.* London: National Curriculum Council.

National Writing Project (1989) *Responding to and Assessing Writing.* London: National Curriculum Council.

National Writing Project (1989) *Audiences for Writing.* London: National Curriculum Council.

National Writing Project (1990) *Perceptions of Writing.* London: National Curriculum Council.

Raban, B. (ed.) (1985) *Practical Ways to Teach Writing.* London: Ward Lock Educational.

Temple, C.A., Nathan, Ruth G. & Burris, Nancy, A. (1982) *The Beginnings of Writing.* Boston: Allyn & Bacon.

Wray, D., Bloom, W. & Hall, N. (1989) *Literacy in Action: The Development of Literacy in the Primary Years.* Lewes: Falmer Press.

CHAPTER 4

MEDIA EDUCATION

Elizabeth Pye

As the media and variety of messages proliferate, so we need to be adept in 'reading' these messages and using the media.

Kingman Report (DES 1988)

Media Education refers to the wide cross-curricular exploration of the media as part of the Primary and Lower Secondary Curriculum. It is thus distinct from *Media Studies* which is generally used to refer to a discrete subject course for older students. In this chapter, we set out to explore:

- the different elements of Media Education and its place in the National Curriculum
- the notion of 'media literacy' and the kinds of issues which children need to understand
- the notion of bias
- the choice of suitable materials
- activities which promote the critical approach which underpins Media Education
- resources for Media Education

What is Media Education?

A photograph is usually looked at, seldom looked into.

Oxfam poster

I've brought the photos I took in Pakistan, Miss
Can I bring my new tape to the party?
We got a great new tape in our language from the video shop last night.

Children are saturated with media images. Film, video, television, books, newspapers, computer software, photography and popular music form a large part of our lives. They have a powerful cumulative effect. When children come to school they bring with them a knowledge of and interest in the media that becomes incorporated into their writing, drawings, discussions and games. However, while the context of the community in late twentieth-century Britain is both multilingual and multicultural, it would be difficult to guess that this is the case from the television or radio. The socially constructed messages presented to us through the media need to be made explicit to children if they are to understand them fully and make their own decisions about legitimacy.

In the past, children's curiosity about the media and their mine of informally-gathered knowledge was largely ignored in schools. The formal recognition of Media Education in the National Curriculum English document therefore opens up exciting possibilities. If children are exposed to the right 'media questions', the opportunities are there for teachers to forge links between home and school, to enable children to explore personal identity, to raise questions about contemporary culture and power structures and to look at alternatives.

Media Education aims to enable children to become active and critical users of the media, rather than passive consumers; to encourage them to question, rather than to simply accept, the messages they receive; to see themselves as capable of making media products on their own terms, taking power over the media themselves; to see the media as a potential agent for change.

The (1989) Cox Report on *English for Ages 5–16,* the British Film Institute (BFI) curriculum statements (Bazalgette 1989; Bowker 1990) and the National Curriculum English document (DES 1988) all agree that Media Education should be built into the work of the modern classroom. The BFI statement on *Primary Media Education* is particularly interesting in this respect. It presents an invaluable, structured approach to the teaching of the media and it is a pity that the recommendation made there that English Attainment Target 1 (Speaking and Listening) should be altered to 'Speaking, Listening and Watching' was not taken up in the final National Curriculum document. Visual literacy appears to take a minor role, though we find suggestions in the Attainment Targets and Programmes of Study which incorporate visual material, such as the following :

- discussing pictures, television, radio, computer
- using appropriate media technology, e.g. video recorders, radio, television
- group and individual work on stories, newspapers, magazines, books, games and guides
- using opportunities to express and justify feelings, opinions, viewpoints

In the absence of more specific guidelines, teachers must draw on their own knowledge and use of structured Media Education concepts to ensure that the opportunities given by activities such as these are used to the full.

Media literacy

'Literacy' is a word that can be used to describe the ability to 'read' words and images. A film, a photograph or a video are usually referred to as 'texts', and can be approached in many similar ways to a written text. There is an important proviso, however. Messages are conveyed through different media. Each one (film, photography, words) uses different technology and conventions to tell a story or convey a message.

Steps in media literacy

Different classroom projects can either draw selectively upon, or make extensive use of, different media. There are, however, many points of contact between the different shapes of literacy, and the ways that they interconnect should be constantly borne in mind and referred to in discussions. Children need to:

- understand that most 'texts' are the result of someone choosing that they should look like that, that they have been deliberately constructed
- identify how the 'text' has been designed, and that there is a viewpoint
- explore why the image was made, who by, who for, and appreciate that this

is important in our understanding of it
- look for bias, omission, simplification or distortion. (Who gets represented? Who doesn't? Which groups are often/hardly ever shown? How are they shown? Are some groups habitually shown in a limited role or as victims?
- identify and challenge stereotypes
- ask questions and challenge situations shown in the media
- recognise the role that feelings and attitudes play in the way we respond to pictures, books, films, etc.
- look for the implications and issues involved

Whose viewpoint?

Starting from an analysis of how pictures, films, articles, etc. are put together and make their meanings, children can explore this question for themselves, using writing or drawing to present information about themselves, moving on to show themselves in a different mood, or as other people see them. In any environment or school ethos, it is important that children should see how they can construct different representations of their own identity in different ways, before they go on to explore the messages which we receive about other people.

If we use materials that reflect a multiracial view of the world, questions and assumptions about race, groups or countries are often raised that can be difficult to answer and challenge if the ground has not been prepared carefully first, especially in monocultural surroundings. But in using the basic knowledge that images are not neutral, it is easier to explore the paths by which we acquire views about other people or events, or look at the role of gender, class and race in determining how images are made.

So questions such as these might arise:

- How would a boy/girl make this advertisement in a different way?
- Is the family in that TV series like my family or other families I know? Who is it aimed at?
- How many advertisements or programmes directly relate to or reflect the interests of Black audiences?
- Are minority groups justly represented on TV? How many Black presenters are there? How can we account for this? Do we want things to change?
- What view of a country do we get from looking at these photographs? Do they show a tourist's or disaster view? Who took them? Would a person from that country take different pictures?
- How has this group been represented historically? Are there economic or political reasons for this?
- Who owns the media? Who is their largest audience? How does this affect the programmes they show?
- How does the way that events or people are shown affect the way we feel about them?

Choosing materials

Look for images that reflect a wider-world perspective. Ask yourself whether they offer an accurate and positive representation of the subject. There are many useful sources for materials of this kind:

- photographs, e.g. the UNICEF diary and the New Internationalist calendar are full of positive multicultural images. Be wary of tourist views or newspaper images of Black people as victims of war or disaster
- postcard reproductions of art, including portraits, sculptures and written materials from different cultures
- newspapers and magazines in different languages (from children, parents, staff, holidays, the local newsagent, etc)
- music – film music, world music, children's favourite tapes. Discuss instruments from different cultures, the Black roots of rock, etc.

Activities

A wide range of activities can be used to encourage the kind of critical approach which underpins media education, including:

Self-portraits

- display a variety of reproductions of portraits (photos, paintings)
- get children to write individually or explain orally what a picture tells us about the sitter (age, job, character, etc.)
- get children to plan and paint or have a photograph taken to convey messages about themselves, such as important things in their lives, hobbies, what type of person they are, favourite colour in clothes

Brainstorming

- photocopy a detailed photograph of a busy scene or group of people and place it in the centre of a large sheet of paper
- in a small group, get children to write as many questions as they can about the photograph around the edge
- discuss the result. What ambiguities did they discover? What wider issues were opened up?

Headlines

- give out several copies of the same photograph to each group. It should be fairly detailed, for example a group of people
- each group should select and cut out a small part of the photograph, stick it on to a larger sheet of paper and write a headline or a caption for it
- discuss how selection and captioning alters the meaning of the image

Viewpoints and audiences

- use a set of newspaper reports about the same event, or a video of TV news reports from different channels reporting the same thing
- ask the children to investigate and compare factual information, vocabulary, pictures, layout, tone

● explore questions of viewpoint, other possible presentations, omissions
● children could go on to write their own versions

Images of people

● make a collection of magazines and newspapers and share them out
● each group should look for and cut out pictures of one of these groups: children, men, women, Black people
● ask them to discuss the pictures. What 'types' in each set can they or can't they find? What do we see these people doing? What don't we see these people doing?

Stereotyping

● collect picture postcards and tourist leaflets about your local area
● discuss the children's own view of their area. Is it the same? What is important to them? What would they show about their lives or area to a visitor?
● get children to make sets of drawings or sets of photographs to show their own viewpoint of the area or to show it in a particular light
● collect pictures of a country outside Europe or North America from newspapers, books, tourist brochures. Look in newspapers aimed at indigenous communities for alternative views.

References

Bazalgette, C. (1989) *Primary Media Education: A Curriculum Statement.* London: British Film Institute Education Department.

Bowker, J. (ed.) (1990) *Secondary Media Education: A Curriculum Statement.* London: British Film Institute Education Department.

Department of Education and Science (1988) *Report of the Committee of Inquiry into the Teaching of English* (The Kingman Report). London: HMSO.

Department of Education and Science (1988) *English National Curriculum 5– 11,* London: HMSO.

Department of Education and Science (DES) (1989) *English for Ages 5 – 16* (The Cox Report). London: DES Welsh Office.

Resources for media education

The teaching of media education

Lusted, D. and Drummond, P. (eds.) (1985) *TV and Schooling.* London: British Film Institute Education Department.

Masterman, L. (1985) *Teaching the Media.* London: Comedia/M.K. Media Press. [Comprehensive study of Media Education].

Resource books and Teaching Packs

Bethel, A. (1981) *Eyeopener One. Eyeopener Two.* Cambridge: Cambridge
   University Press. [Activities to introduce image analysis, narrative, news
   photographs, documentaries and advertisements. Accompanying
   photographs also available. Suitable for secondary level]

Birmingham Development Centre (1990) *What is a Family?*
   [From: Birmingham Development Centre, Selly Oak Cottages, Bristol
   Road, Birmingham B29 6LE. Photo-activity pack about family life in the
   UK]

Davies, Y. (1986) *Picture Stories.* London: British Film Institute Education
   Department. [Image Study Pack. Suitable for primary level]

Davies, Y. (1979) *Reading Pictures.* London: British Film Institute Education
Department. [Image Analysis pack. Suitable for third and fourth year secondary
   level]

Davies, Y. (1983) *Selling Pictures.* London: British Film Institute Education
   Department. [Representation and stereotyping. Suitable for secondary level]

Fisher, D. and Hicks, D. (1985) *World Studies 8–13.* Edinburgh: Oliver and Boyd.
   [Practical resource book on wider world activities]

Fuirer, M. (ed.) (1989) *Whose Image? Anti-Racist Approaches to Photography
   and Visual Literacy.* London: Building Sights.

Hornsby, J. (ed.) (1989) *Photography: Towards a Multicultural Approach.*
   South East Arts amd East Sussex County Council. [Report of activities
   undertaken during East Sussex 'Photography in Schools' project.]

McFarlane, C. (1986) *Hidden Messages? Activities for Exploring Bias.*
   Development Education Centre, Selly Oak Cottages, Bristol Road,
   Birmingham B29 6LE.

Thomas, P. (undated) Images: A Resource Pack. London: The Woodcraft
   Folk, 13 Ritherdon Road, London SW17 8QE. [Activities exploring race,
   gender and other countries]

Manchester Development Education Project (1988) *Watching the World.*
   (1) Investigating Images: Working with pictures on an International
   Theme. (2) News from Nicaragua: Fact and Fiction (3) Aspects of Africa:
   Questioning perceptions (4) Picturing People: Challenging Stereotypes (5)
   "Whose news?": Ownership and Control of the News Media (simulation
   game). Manchester Development Education Project, c/o Manchester
   Polytechnic, 801 Wilmslow Road, Manchester M20 8RG. [Five studies of
   the influence of the media on images, perceptions and values we hold about
   the countries and peoples of the world. For the 13–15 age range but can be
   adapted for younger children]

A variety of **photographic packs,** for example, The Visit, The Station, The
Fairground, The Market, are available for work on narrative and montage from
SEFT, 29 Old Compton Street, London W1V 5PL.

Catalogues containing useful material for use in Media Education are available
from:

British Film Institute, Education Department, 21 Stephen Street, London W1P 1PL.

Centre for World Development Education, Regents College, Inner Circle, Regents Park, London NW1 4NS.

Oxfam, 274 Banbury Road, Oxford OX2 7DZ.

Society for Education in Film and Television Ltd., 29 Old Compton Street, London W1V 5PL.

Part Two

The Case Studies

CHAPTER 5

THEY DON'T HAVE ANY BLACK PEOPLE IN THE BOOK

Jagiro Goodwin and Angela Wellings

The following case study falls into three sections:

- the first describes the background and preparation necessary to engage pupils in critical debate
- the second suggests strategies for assisting pupils to become active participants in the review of their school library
- the last section highlights supportive materials and resources for extension work

The school: community and ethos

The primary school described in the following case study serves an urban community that is socially and racially mixed. Approximately a third of the pupils are from families of Asian and African-Caribbean origin. As a result there is a tremendous variety of languages, dialects and cultures represented within the school.

The school views this variety as a positive educational and social resource as it strives to ensure that its pupils become self-confident young people who are able to 'recognise prejudice and deal with it in a manner that is based on concern for others. Within the school there is a strong commitment to education for racial equality which underpins not only what is taught but also staff development, recruitment and general school organisation.

The context for the project

In the autumn term 1989 the staff evaluated its initiatives to date on education for racial equality and devised a new plan for further action.

One iniative identified in the new plan was the evaluation and update of the library. The Humanities section was the starting point as this was the subject area most prone to stereotyping. The school's project on weather had also alerted staff to the fact that this section housed many negative resources showing the developing world in the grip of famine, flood or drought.

We were given the responsibility for the evaluation and it was not long before we made the decision that it would be challenging for both ourselves and the pupils to be engaged in the task together. We hoped that the involvement would raise their awareness of racial bias and stereotyping in texts and make them more active critics of the books they read. We wanted also to work towards arriving at a set of mutually agreed criteria, that the pupils across the school could use to detect such bias and stereotyping. As the subject matter was controversial and sensitive and one to which discussion and debate would be central, careful preparation was crucial.

The pupils

The pupils involved in the project were a mixed ability group from the 5th and 6th year classes. Each week we worked with a different group of twelve pupils, 4 from each class, enabling us to work with seventy-two pupils in all.

Building trust and confidence

Many of the pupils involved in the activity had never worked together before. As the main task was to engage the pupils in a great deal of discussion on controversial issues, it was essential to begin with building confidence and trust within the group. The ability to listen and to take turns would also be important. With these considerations in mind, we engaged the pupils in the following exercises, having of course first outlined the overall aim of the project to them.

The magic microphone

This exercise is very effective as an 'ice breaker'. The group forms a circle and one person is given an object which serves as a microphone. The person with the microphone speaks for a specified amount of time (agreed before hand by the group) on any topic or issue of her/his choice, whilst the rest of the group listens. The microphone is then passed on until each person in the group has had a turn to speak. In our case, we agreed that each member of the group would spend one minute telling us something about themselves. Not as easy as it sounds! Some pupils were initially very reluctant to be the first to speak, in which case one of us began. The pupils were encouraged by our risk taking and soon even the most reluctant pupil was eager to participate. The listening aspect of the exercise was reinforced by each pupil recalling one or two points about someone else in the group.

Other possibilities for confidence and trust building

Consequences: This exercise is a variation of that timeless game well known to generations of young people. The group forms a circle and each person writes their name at the bottom of a sheet of paper and passes it to the neighbour sitting to their right. The neighbour writes something positive about the person at the top, folds the paper down and passes it to the next person who also writes an affirming comment, folds the paper down and passes it on. The sheet of paper finally returns to the owner with a number of positive comments about them from the group.

My name: Individuals in the group talk about their name and how they feel about it, who named them and why they were given that particular name.

Developing listening skills

The children were asked to get into pairs. Each pupil was given a black and white photograph with the instruction not to disclose it to their partner. In each pair, one partner described her/his photograph, whilst the other partner drew the contents. The exercise was repeated with the partners swapping roles. At the end of the exercise the partners compared their drawings and photographs for accurate listening and verbal description.

Other listening activities

Whispers: This is another well known game which can be used to develop listening skills. The pupils sit in a circle and someone whispers a sentence to her/his neighbour who whispers it to the next person until it comes back to the original source. Sentences of varying length can be tried. If the whisper becomes distorted on its journey around the group an interesting discussion can take place on whether some words or phrases get more easily distorted than others and why this might be so. A list of things which help people hear words correctly could also be made.

Listening time: Pupils are asked to listen for one minute to any sounds coming from outside the room. They then say what they heard. This is an effective way to begin a session as it helps to focus attention on the 'here and now.' It also illustrates the different interpretations of sounds and leads to questions about the importance of evidence.

Brainstorming

If we were to assist pupils in learning to detect bias and stereotypes in books, we needed to begin with a knowledge of the stereotypes they already possessed. It would be naive to assume that our pupils were somehow immune to the influences of the wide world. We explained to the pupils that we were going to do some brainstorming and described it for those who didn't know what this would entail. In order to make the task readily accessible we began with a brainstorm on the popular television soap opera from Australia, 'Neighbours.' Much of the brainstorm was a list of the characters and issues being raised by the programme at the time, such as divorce, boyfriend /girlfriend relationships, marriage and so on.

This was immediately followed by a brainstorm on 'The continent of Africa.' This time the pupils in all our groups consistently articulated many more crude stereotypes. To them this vast continent represented the list recorded by a member of the group and reproduced on page 74.

It was interesting to note that out of all our groups, only one child responded to the brainstorm with a non-stereotyped comment. He was an African-Caribbean child to whom Africa symbolized Nelson Mandela.

The brainstorming enabled us to lead into and sustain a lengthy discussion on such questions as:

● What is a stereotype?
● What kinds of stereotypes are there?
● Where do stereotypes come from and how do we learn them?

Africa is ....

weapons

pythons   poor people

dry   Spears

Tarzan

drought

war in Ethiopia
elephants

starvation

Often the pupils arrived at answers to these questions in circuitous and interesting ways. In attempting to define the various stereotypes that exist one group engaged in an animated discussion on caricatures in the television satire, 'Spitting Image.' The pupils discussed how the programme used negative physical features and personal habits as a basis for ridicule. This led into a discussion of racial caricatures where the pupils began to see parallels between the techniques used on a programme such as 'Spitting Image' and artists' caricatures of non-White people. Some of them had observed that Chinese people were often portrayed as 'slant or slit-eyed' and Africans as 'thick-lipped and wielding spears'. There was general agreement that these portrayals led to negative stereotypes being held.

Having built up the trust and confidence of the pupils, we were able to use the brainstorming as a springboard for the main activity which followed.

Evaluating the books

The group was t asked to do the next activity in pairs. Each pair was given a book from the Humanities section of the library. We tried to ensure that there was a balance of books reflecting both positive and negative images so that the feedback session would provide an opportunity for the pupils to compare the materials and to evaluate what is a 'negative' book and what is a 'positive' one. The groups were then asked to spend about forty minutes evaluating the books using a questionnaire to help them. Before this we had gone over the format and the content of the questionnaire to make sure it was comprehensible to everyone. We tried, wherever possible, to pair pupils who needed support with reading with partners who were independent readers.

```
Title of book:.........................................
```

Look carefully at

```
   * the illustrations
   * the text
```

then write your comments about the book in the boxes below.

	Positive	Negative
Facial features		
Dress		
Housing		
Rich/poor		
Relationships with white people		
Language: the words used to describe black people		

Other observations: Are any groups of people missing from the book? If so, who are they and why do you think they have been left out?

Adapting the activity

- the questionnaire could be simplified or adapted to the specific needs of your group or class
- the group could design and produce their own questionnaire
- a matrix could be devised, where ticks or crosses would obviate the need for as much writing to be done

---

Each pair then spent the first five minutes or so scanning the book to get a 'flavour' of its contents. What followed next was the main part of the activity, where the pairs examined the books using the questionnaire as a supportive framework. This activity was particularly exciting. As we moved around the room we could hear the pupils engaging in quite heated discussion.

They argued, showed disapproval when materials were especially negative, negotiated at quite a sophisticated level and, in most cases, reached a consensus about their books. Although the feedback session was to be very important, the interaction which took place before it showed how the pupils were becoming increasingly aware of the collaborative aspect of the activity. They involved each other in discussion, listened and considered alternative opinions and, where necessary, provided counter-arguments. As English 5–16 (DES, 1989) states:

> The effectiveness of talking and listening is determined not only by the ability to use speech appropriately, but also by the ability to listen actively.

The feedback

The group came back together towards the end of the session to report on their findings. We formed a large circle once more and invited one member of each pair in turn to describe their book to the rest of the group while one of the teachers acted as a 'scribe' on a flipchart. As a general rule, books containing photographs were viewed more positively than those containing illustrations. The illustrations in one particular book, *This is China* were found by the pupils to be caricatures and many comments were made about this book causing offence:

> All the faces look the same.

> The book makes everyone look the same.

> It's not true that Chinese people have yellow skin because you can't have yellow skin.

Similarly, books which portrayed only *one perspective* were criticised:

> This book shows that people in England are rich and that's not true.

The pupils also detected *bias by omission*. They commented that some of the books portrayed only one group of people and ignored the other groups living in that country, for example:

People at work in Bangladesh were left out.

Books which called certain groups by *inaccurate and offensive names* were highlighted. The pupils were critical of one particular book entitled *The Indians of the Crow Tribe* and much fruitful discussion followed where they compared the situation in North America with Australia's treatment of Aboriginal peoples and questioned the appropriateness of the book's title:

I think the book has a title that almost fits as it says what the book is about but the title should be changed because they are not really Indians; they are Native Americans.

Extending the activity

Pupils could discuss why:

- photographs generally are more positive than illustrations
- authors often present a one-sided view of a particular country or people
- it is important to call people by accurate names

Adapting the activity

This activity could be adapted to examine issues relating to:

- gender
- disability
- age

Looking back

Each group reached very similar conclusions about the books they had evaluated. One of the books, *This is China*, provoked a very angry response from almost all the pupils, who claimed it should be removed forthwith from the library before it caused any more offence. With such an overtly biased book, of course, it was easier for the pupils to recognise this bias at once. What was more difficult for them to recognise was covert bias in some of the books. For instance one book *Families around the World*, at first glance appeared quite a positive one since it seemed to reflect black and white families in roughly equal proportions. On closer inspection, however, it was found to present a very one-sided view of families in non-European countries.

One group commented:

> Most people in Africa and Asia are shown in rags and living in slums... There's only one picture showing a rich family in Asia...

The activity ended with a final discussion about what should happen to the books. We operated a voting system, whereby if the majority of the group found a book offensive and believed it had no place in the school library, then it was agreed it should be removed.

Extending the activity

Pupils could be encouraged to:

- devise a 'book-look' system to alert others that particular books should be read with caution

- develop their own set of criteria for selecting materials; (there are many useful guidelines to use as stimuli, such as those of the World Council of Churches (see Preiswerk 1980)

- write to the authors/publishers/illustrators concerned, in protest at offensive material

---

One of the initial aims of the project was to reach, with the pupils, an agreed set of criteria for evaluating books and other materials. Unfortunately, lack of time prevented this being achieved. Nevertheless, the activity itself was an extremely worthwhile one to undertake as it sensitized the pupils to the important concerns of bias and stereotyping, and left them more able to make informed decisions about the positive and negative aspects of books.

This kind of project could be done in any school, whether racially-mixed or not. What is of crucial importance, however, is to ensure that the ethos of the school is one which will enable this type of work to take place. A great deal of preparation and ground work is needed to reach a stage whereby pupils can respond positively to the exploration of such controversial issues. The section which follows highlights several invaluable resources which will help teachers in this preparation work, by offering practical ideas and strategies, which can be used in a variety of classroom settings.

Selected resources for follow-up activities

Introduction

This section highlights a number of useful resources which challenge stereotypes and inequalities and provide the teacher with plenty of practical suggestions for classroom activities.

What is a Family? Devleopment Education Centre, Birmingham.

This black and white photopack depicting families living in Britain today is particularly good for raising issues of race, gender and disability stereotyping. It also looks at family structures such as marriage, single parents and childless families. Gender roles and children's roles are explored. The pack is designed to be used with children and young people aged 8 and above, as well as with adults. It is very useful in INSET work.

There are many follow-up activities arising from this pack. One that works especially well is a 'Happy Families' game, made using the children's drawings of their own families. Each child in the group draws individual pictures of four people in their family, including themselves. The game proves very popular, not only with the children concerned but also with other children who recognise their friends from the drawings.

Working Now. Brent Curriculum Development Service Unit.

This is another black and white photopack. The photographs represent working women and men in non-traditional roles. The accompanying teachers' booklet is divided into four sections: discussion, drama, writing and extension activities.
Working Now is an excellent resource for exploring attitudes to work and to gender issues. The suggested extension activities involve collaborative work such as interviewing staff and children, devising questionnaires and interpreting data, and evaluating books.

In addition to raising serious issues and providing opportunities for children to discuss these in depth, the activities are interesting and engaging. For example, in a mixed group of ten and eleven year olds where we used these materials, one of the activities stimulated a very heated discussion about the photograph of the electrician. The boys were convinced the worker was a man (because of the short hair). The girls in the group disputed this by asking how many women the boys knew with very short hair, including teachers and mothers, finally getting the boys to admit that they had assumed the job could only be done by a man.

Another group had a great deal of fun inventing amusing names for workers and produced a book of their 'characters', including 'Mr Markitright' the teacher and 'Ms Plier' the dentist.

Nowhere to play by Kurusa

Nowhere to Play is a well-illustrated story, set in a shantytown, Barrio San José, in the hills above Caracas in Venezuela. It tells the true story of a group of children living in San José and their struggle to find a playground. The children were so tired of having no play area that they petitioned their local council, had their plight reported in the local press and persuaded their parents and other adults to support them. The council eventually agreed to set aside a stretch of waste ground for the playground to be built. For months nothing happened. Finally the children and adults of San José took matters into their own hands and decided to build the playground themselves.

Not only is the story excellent for sharing with children of all ages, it can be used as a stimulus for developing a wide range of activities in a variety of curriculum areas, as the flowchart on page 81, prepared by Saroj Mistry, demonstrates.

The Sea People by J. Steiner and J. Muller.

This beautifully illustrated book relates the mythical tale of two islands and their inhabitants. The larger of the two islands comprises a community which is highly stratified, motivated by a strong work ethic and governed by an avaricious king. As a complete contrast, the smaller island has no ruler, the people have equality and live very simply in peace and harmony. The story revolves around the eventual destruction of the larger island which is brought about by the king's greed and selfishness.

One of the most obvious strengths of this book is its stunning illustrations which engage children of all ages. The story itself, however, is an excellent vehicle for raising many serious concerns such as:

- migration
- colonization
- industrialization
- slavery
- resistance
- empathy
- destruction

Issues and concerns

◆ Idea of home — Zeynep by ALTARF

◆ Destruction of space

◆ Rapid change and growth
 – effects on environment
 – wider issue of deforestation & desertification

Science A.T.9 A.T. 3

◆ Colonisation – impact on local community e.g. family life, resources

◆ Resistance as a powerful tool for positive change

◆ Concepts of powerful and power less, just and unjust, fair and unfair

Mathematics A.T. 14:3:3
Science A.T. 1:3:3

◆ Commonality of struggles of children and minority groups

Science A.T. 2:3/4

Suitable projects

✤ Ourselves
✤ Our Community
✤ Our Environment
✤ Movement/Migration
✤ Change/Growth
✤ Homes
✤ Families

Other Resources

✤ For full details see page 101
✤ The Sea People
✤ Zeynep – That really happened to me
✤ Games of the World
✤ The Art of Play
✤ Five Stones and Knuckle Bones
✤ Let's Cooperate

Nowhere to Play

by Kurusa,
A & C Black, 1982

Art and Technology

✤ Design campaign posters
✤ Design a play area
✤ Make a 3D model
✤ Design and paint a mural
✤ Paint games on the ground

Maths, Science, English

Science

❖ Investigate suitability of play area
 – safety
 – type of soil
 – natural habitats of animals
 – any weather conditions
 – traffic and noise factors, transport and accessibility

Science
A.T. 5:3/5 A.T. 9:2:2

Language and Drama

Can be approached through discussion, drama and role play, and/or writing

● Storytelling – by pupils/teacher
● Predicting – from title; telling the story in parts

English   A.T. 2:4/5
Mathematics A.T. 1:2:3
                      1:3:4

● Idea of encroaching on space
● Points of view representing an argument from different perspectives

Science   A.T. 5:5:3

● Using various media for presenting your perspective – radio, T.V., newspaper reports, letters, posters
● Interview people invovled in local projects – organisers, the children who use the facilities

Mathematics

◯ Survey to identify the most suitable local spot for a play area
 – devise a questionnaire
 – collect information
 – present information in various forms

Maths, Science English

Mathematics
A.T. 11, 12, 13

Use of computer for recording findings

– cost of equipment, paint, etc.

As well as providing opportunities for children to engage in debate surrounding the issues outlined above, the book stimulates many ideas for extension activities in various curriculum areas such as Technology, Science and Maths.

References

Birmingham Development Education Centre (1985) *What Is A Family?* Birmingham Development Education Centre.

Brent Curriculum Development Service Unit (CDSU) (1984). *Working Now.* Birmingham Development Education Centre.

Department of Education and Science (DES) (1989) *English for Ages 5–16.* London: DES and Welsh Office.

Deshapande, C (1988) *Five Stones and Knucklebones.* London: A. and C. Black.

Fisher, S and Hicks, D. (1985) *World Studies 8–13.* A Teacher's Handbook. Edinburgh: Oliver and Boyd.

Hasbudak, Z and Simons, B. (undated) *Zeynep – That really happened to me.* London: ALTARF.

Kurusa (1982) *Nowhere to Play.* London: A. and C. Black.

Masheder, M. (1986) *Let's Cooperate.* London: Peace Education Project.

Preiswerk, R. (1980) *Racism in Children's Books.* Geneva: World Council of Churches.

Reed, K. (ed) (1985) *The Art of Play.* London: CSV and Ethnographic Resources for Art Education.

Steiner, J and Muller, J. (1982) *The Sea People.* London: Gollancz.

UNICEF (1982) *Games of the World.* London: UNICEF.

Other Books and Material.

Dixon, B. (1978) *Catching Them Young.* (2 Volumes). London: Pluto Press.

Epstein, D and Sealey, A. (1990) *"Where it really matters..."* Birmingham Development Education Centre.

Klein, G. (1985) *Reading Into Racism.* Bias in Children's Literature and Learning Materials. London: Routledge.

Milner, D. (1983) *Children and Race Ten Years On.* London: Ward Lock Educational.

Twitchen, J. (ed) (1988) *The Black and White Media Book.* Stoke-on-Trent: Trentham Books.

CHAPTER 6

"I am glad you wrote this book"

Saroj Mistry

Zeynep - That really happened to me is a true story about a Turkish family's experience of deportation from their home in Hackney, London. It documents the sustained campaign of protest and challenge by school children, teachers, friends, workmates and members of the community. The story is by Zeynep, the eight year old daughter in the Hasbudak family, and Brian Simons, her teacher. It takes a number of different forms – a descriptive narrative, a diary, letters and photographs.

Sadly the campaign failed and the family were forced to leave their friends and life in Britain. For all involved, however, the deportation raised important issues relating to the injustice of a racist law which divides families.

In partnership with the class teacher, I used this story with 7–9 year olds in an environment which encouraged discussion and mutual respect. This was very much in keeping with the ethos of the school which aimed, among other things, to foster an atmosphere of purposeful learning and exciting challenges, and where cultural diversity was seen as a valuable resource.

Context for the project

All too often, work which focuses on the experiences of Black people and raises issues of injustice and racism, is 'tagged on' and bears little relevance to the rest of the curriculum being delivered in the classroom. This has the effect of both giving the issues low status and creating more work for the teacher. For these reasons, it was important that work on *Zeynep* formed an integral part of other classroom activities. As the school topic was on 'Ourselves' and the children were already engaged in gathering information on their own autobiographies, there was no danger of marginalization. Zeynep's forced exile was further supported by work on *Anne Frank's Diary* which also deals with the question of enforced hiding.

Aims

I wanted to use Zeynep's story to explore a number of different issues, including:

- the concepts of belonging, home, family, power and powerlessness
- the rights of individuals to choose where they live
- what it means to be exiled or deported

It was also important that children should feel empowered to take positive action in threatening situations such as exile and deportation.

Activities

The work on Zeynep took place one morning a week over a period of six weeks. Discussion played a central role throughout this time, but children were also engaged in a wide range of activities which included brainstorming and then classifying the ideas generated by the brainstorm, letter writing and role play.

Two activities were particularly successful in enabling pupils to express genuine concern for the plight of the Hasbudak family and in broadening their understanding of issues such as justice and injustice, power and powerlessness.

These activities are described below.

Dear Brian Simons ....

Thursday the 5th,

Dear Brian Simons,

my name is Louise. I am 8 years old.
The stroy is very interesting Because of
the Pictures and how you and Zeynep
wrote it, I did'nt exPect it to haPPened in
this country and I am very sad it
did haPPened. The story is a little sad
and a little happy. But I did'nt think
the world could Be so cruel, I am
sorry it happned to zeyneP, The story is
very good,
Zeyzep was very brave, I like your Book
very much, But it hurts inside to Know that
it haPPened in real life, The children and every
one did all they could But what they did
Was not a enough to stoP zeyzep and her
family to stay. I hope you like my
Letter.

love from Louise chandler

P.S. Please Write Back.

organize non-chronological writing for different purposes in orderly ways.
[Attainment Target 3: Writing, level 4c]

write in a variety of forms for a range of purposes and audiences, in ways
which attempt to engage the interest of the reader.
[Attainment Target 3: Writing, level 5a]

The first activity involved the pupils in writing letters to Brian Simons who still teaches at Zeynep's old school and is in regular contact with the family. Every child wanted to write, so much so that children who were absent on the day were eager to write letters on their return to school. Their letters expressed outrage at the injustice of Zeynep's deportation, feelings of solidarity with the family and a genuine concern to know the family's whereabouts today. One letter in particular , reproduced on page 85, encapsulates the children's concerns.

Role play

participate in a presentation
[Attainment Target 1: Speaking and Listening, level 4d]

take part as speakers and listeners in a group discussion or activity, expressing a personal view and commenting constructively on what is being discussed.
[Attainment Target 1: Speaking and Listening, level 4c]

The second activity involved the children in role play where they had to represent particular individuals and groups involved with Zeynep's family and their case. They were asked to assume the roles of the Hasbudak family, the family's friends, neighbours, people at work and the Home Secretary. Each group or individual prepared and presented their case for or against the deportation of Zeynep and her family. My attention was drawn to the readiness with which the children assumed role and their sensitivity to body language. The speed with which they realised the strength and resolve of bureaucratic power was also striking. Comments in the discussion which followed, such as:

We were not getting through. It felt unreal

You sounded like you were making excuses because you were wrong and we were right and you didn't want to admit it

further highlighted their critical awareness of power relationships and, in the context of Zeynep's story, gave rise to new ideas on how the problem facing the family could be resolved.

Possible extension activities

The activities involved in this particular project by no means exhausted the range of possibilities. I have tried to illustrate on the flow chart opposite some of the ways in which the work could be extended. I have also attempted to highlight additional resources which raise issues similar to those in Zeynep's story.

ZEYNEP – That really happened to me (Hasbudak & Simons)

Suitability
Across the primary sector,
Infants & Juniors

Topics or Themes
Ourselves   Books
Migration   Families
Movement   Travel
Journeys   Media
Homes   Communications

Curriculum Areas
English/Language
Modern Languages
Drama/Dance/Movement
Geography
History
Art – Visual
Mathematics

Issues
Justice & Fairness
Belonging   Valuables
Freedom   Protest
Power   Bias
Racism   Citizenship
Deportation   Breaking the Law
Right to Choose   Right & Wrong
What is "British?"

Useful Resources
(For full details see page 88)
What is a Family? (Development
Education Centre 1985)
Moving On (Gerlach et al. 1987)
Ourselves (ACER 1981)
Let's Co-operate (Masheder 1986)
Nowhere to Play (Karusa 1982)
The Sea People (Müller & Steiner 1982)
A Place to Stay (Age Exchange 1984)

Activities
Role play – telling the story through different individuals and groups; two teams, For and
Against staying; witnesses; character reference
Letter writing to...
Letter writing from...
Survey (class, school) of where people are from, the languages they speak...
Reasons for moving house – what you leave behind & look forward to
My family is... or *My Family means...to me* or *The best things about my family are...*
My home is... or *My home means... to me*
Sorting a list of statements in order of importance – reasons why the family should stay
Investigate any local cases of deportation – media coverage, bias or perspective;
presentation through storytelling, drama visual exhibition
Organise a petition and publicity for something of importance in own school/locality which
would give a sense of power to bring about change
Design banners and posters; draw up a plan of action; keep a diary
Mapwork
Plotting Zeynep's journeys; plotting personal journeys
Personal timeline, family timeline
Dance/Movement expression of experiences, feelings, relationships

References

Afro-Caribbean Educational Resources Project (ACER)(1981) *Ourselves*. London: ACER.

Age Exchange Theatre Company (1984) *A Place to Stay*. London: Age Exchange Theatre Company.

Development Education Centre (1985) *What is a Family?* Birmingham: Development Education Centre.

Frank, A. (1989) *Anne Frank's Diary*. London: Pan.

Gerlach, L., Hillier, S. Bennett, J. and Hearty, D. (1987) *Moving On*. London: Minority Rights Group.

Hasbudak, Z. & Simons, B. (undated) *Zeynep - That Really Happened to Me*. London: ALTARF.

Masheder, M. (1986) *Let's Cooperate*. London: Peace Education Project.

Müller, J. & Steiner, J. (1982) *The Sea People*. London: Gollancz.

CHAPTER 7

"It's not like what we usually do"

Sheena Vick

The work that the artist has done is certainly different from what we normally do in art.

It was really good. She wasn't like I thought artists would be, she had her own ideas and she used her own experiences.

I find it more difficult talking about myself and then putting it into a picture as a story of my life. I have never done anything like this before so it is a bit harder than normal art lessons.

Bisakha came from Liverpool to show us how to dance.

These are examples of comments made by pupils after working with visual artists, dancers, crafts-people, storytellers, writers and musicians. They indicate the amount of thought, discussion and enjoyment which arose out of seeing artists at work and from working alongside them. Artists not only bring with them the skills and approaches concerned with their art form. They also bring new ideas and a fresh vocabulary which can enable pupils to develop their own ideas into a creative form.

The Context

As an LEA co-odinator for the Arts Education for a Multicultural Society (AEMS) project, my task was to assist teachers to develop projects which promote the work of Black artists in schools through the setting up of residencies and so to broaden the curriculum to incorporate arts from a non-European background.

In all of the projects, planning was crucial to success. My role was to support and facilitate this process. Discussion took place over a term leading up to the residency itself and involved both artists and teachers. Evaluation was also an important feature in that it helped to form the projects as they developed and gave teachers, pupils and artists an opportunity to review the impact of the residency on their work.

I have selected two case studies to look at in more depth:

- Bisakha Sarker, a dancer, who worked with a group of 5–11 year olds at a special school
- Allan De Souza, a visual artist and Leena Dhingra, a writer, working with a group of Year 9 pupils in a secondary school

In the various residencies that I have observed, I have been consistently impressed by the added stimulus of an artist who inspires both the pupils and the teacher. Children spent a lot of time talking with the artists, with their teachers and with their friends. They talked about the skills and the processes involved, they explored different ideas and weighed up alternatives; they were keen to volunteer information on what they had learned and what they had liked or disliked. The work with artists also led to lengthy discussions about important issues such as justice and equality and about personal experiences of migration and separation.

In the following case studies I would like to explore the variety of ways in which the arts can be used as a vehicle for developing language skills and, in particular, the ways in which visual artists, crafts-people, story-tellers, writers, dancers and musicians can strengthen and enrich this process. I will look at the practical activities which artists and teachers introduced and at the literacy and oracy work which led to, and arose out of, the practical activities, each strengthening and re-enforcing the other.

'Bisakha came from Liverpool and taught us how to dance'

Artist :	Bisakha Sarker
Artform:	Dance
School:	Special, ages 3–18
Pupils:	The pupils' abilities covered a very wide range, intellectually and physically
Residency:	6 days over 3 weeks

Aims

Until discussion about the project began, dance had not been taught at the school. This project was seen to be the springboard from which dance could be incorporated into the curriculum, both as a subject in itself and as a vehicle through which a whole range of skills and ideas could be taught.

The broad aims of the project were:

- to introduce dance into the school curriculum
- to enable pupils of all abilities to gain some dance skills
- to encourage pupils to work together on a joint activity
- to increase pupils' coordination and physical dexterity
- to develop pupils' listening and speaking skills
- to incorporate and give value to different cultural backgrounds

The artist

Bisakha was herself trained in a variety of classical Indian dance techniques which then formed the foundation for her contemporary style. She introduced a range of Indian dance styles to the pupils who could then use them to create their own dance.

Bisakha used storytelling both as a means of capturing the pupils' imagination and also as a narrative upon which to base the dance. She drew on a range of stories from around the world and invited the pupils to tell their own stories which she then helped them translate into movement. Bisakha also taught the pupils to make small props such as paper flowers, birds and boats which were then used as a part of the dance.

Activities

The project incorporated a number of activities and helped children to develop a range of skills:

- name games - Bisakha's name was one which was unfamiliar to most of the pupils. She knew it would be no good writing her name on the board since not all of the pupils could read. Consequently, she created a number of games where the pupils were required to use her name repeatedly and in a number of contexts.
- say Hello to Dance - Bisakha presented a sequence of dance movements in which all pupils, whatever their mobility, could participate. This sequence was always used at the start of a dance.
- performance - Bisakha danced for the pupils
- symbols - Bisakha taught the pupils particular movements and positions which represent particular things or feelings, for example, a movement to represent an elephant or a flower. Bisakha would introduce a movement and ask the pupils what they thought it might mean and then they would try to do it themselves. In some cases they 'invented' their own movements.
- telling stories - Bisakha would 'tell' a story with words and dance, using the movements the pupils learnt to illustrate the story.
- making a story - Pupils made their own stories which they illustrated with the movements they had learnt and invented.
- making props - Bisakha showed the pupils how to make simple props with folded paper.
- performance - Jonothan told his story to parents and pupils while the rest of the group illustrated it with their dance.

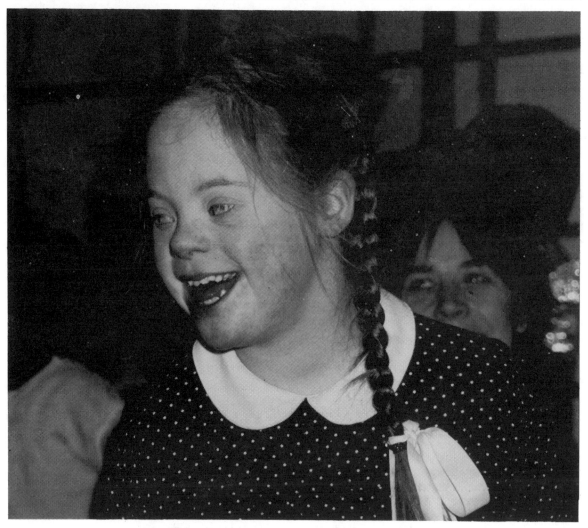

Achievements

● participation - All pupils, whatever their disabilities, were able to join in the dance whether it be with their eyes, their hands or feet or indeed any part of their bodies, each joining in the dance in their own way and each learning new skills in the process.

● dance skills - pupils were in no doubt about what Bisakha had taught them. "I learnt:

.. to make flowers with my hands
.. to wear bells on my feet
.. to be an elephant
.. to say hello to dance
.. to pretend to sleep"

● telling stories - the use of movement and dance to illustrate and to re-tell a story is extremely effective. It helps pupils to remember the story but it also enables them to communicate things which they may find difficult to put into words. The pupils were quick to learn the movements and keen to invent their own, to create their own dance vocabulary.

Bisakha said to me you have a story to tell and I did and they all clapped.

● performance - the project culminated in a performance which the pupils clearly enjoyed. It also provided them, of course, with an opportunity to work together in a purposeful way. In the words of some teachers -

The performance highlighted what the children could do. We too often see them in terms of what they can't do.

It was wonderful to see how pupils could sustain their interest and perform in such a graceful way.
And in the words of one pupil, as he kissed the photograph of the dancer
- I loved Bisakha.d Bisakha.

My Many Selves

Artists:	Allan de Souza and Leena Dhingra
Artforms:	Visual art (collage) and literature
School:	mixed comprehensive
Pupils:	Year 9
Residency:	6 days over 6 weeks

Aims

The two departments, English and Art, decided to work on the theme of 'Self and Self-Image'. Some, but not all, of the pupils would have the opportunity to work with both artists. The school and the LEA have a policy of Education for Racial Equality which includes reviewing the curriculum. Thus, the two departments were keen to identify ways in which they could further extend their curriculum through residencies of Black artists.

The aims of the project were to:

● promote the school policy of Education for Racial Equality in the English and the Arts curriculum
● develop cross-curricular links between the Art and English departments
● produce writing and art work which meets the requirements of the National Curriculum.

The artists

Allan de Souza is a mixed media artist working mainly with photocopy and paint. His work focuses on contemporary Britain, often contrasted with early childhood memories. Allan showed slides of his work, which looked at experiences of racism, and worked in the classroom alongside the pupils.

Leena Dhingra is a writer. She has published a novel, *Amritvela,* (Women's Press, 1988) and has also contributed to an anthology, *Watchers and Seekers* (Women's Press 1987). Leena read from one of her short stories which explored the idea of learning about and understanding oneself.

Activities

The project involved pupils in a number of activities in English and Art lessons:

Presentations. Both artists presented and talked about their own art work, Allan through slides and Leena through reading from her novel, stories and poetry.
Discussions. Pupils were given the opportunity to ask questions of the artists and talk about the artists' work.
Understanding the artists work. Pupils were asked to write about Allan's work, explaining what they liked or disliked, what they found easy or difficult and their own understanding of what he was trying to achieve.
Brainstorming. Leena read one of her short stories, *The Girl Who Didn't Know Herself*. This led to a brainstorming activity where pupils were asked to note how they behaved or responded to different groups of people in different situations.
Letterwriting. Using the brainstorming activity as a source of ideas the pupils were asked to write a letter to a new friend describing themselves. (See the letter to Nicola reproduced opposite).

- *Writing stories* - again using the brainstorming activity as a source of ideas.
- *Writing poetry*
- *Research*. Pupils were asked to collect photographs and objects about themselves and their history.
- *Drawing*   - portraits of friends drawn from touch
                - portraits of friends drawn from memory
                - portraits of self drawn from memory

These drawings were then put on display and pupils were asked to guess who they were.

- *Composition*. Pupils were asked to build a collage which made a statement about themselves, using the material they collected in their research and the ideas they had discussed for their writing. (See the collage and accompanying writing by My-Anh Tran-Dang on page 96).

Dear Nicola,

Recently I have learnt a lot about myself feeling new emotions and finding out that I'm not really the person I thought I was. I'm told in all of us there is more than one person and for me this is terribly confusing. I feel I'm five or six different people all with different values and different personalities.

I've found that when I'm alone I'm very withdrawn and quiet and able to be myself, my real self with no-one to impress and no-one to hold back from. Yet this feeling is not with me for long as I'm hardly ever alone and usually with my friends. Ah! with my friends I'm so different and feel I have to blend with everyone else and entertain them also. I often relax with my friends, yet feel this is not enough and as if I'm not worth anything to my friends. My home life is relaxed and I have no-one to prove myself to, yet I still feel pressurised it's a hard emotion to describe, although I need to tell someone to release me from the torture of not knowing who I am, and what I will end up being.

I often feel lonely even though many people may be surrounding me; this occurs mainly at school where I try so hard to control myself that I push everyone away from me. I then see what I've done and try to regain their attention by doing something out of the ordinary, thus usually finding myself in trouble.

There is only one time that I feel totally fulfilled in my hopes and dreams and this is when I am at rest with myself and full of dreams and aspirations. I am a totally fresh and reliable person at this time and I could fight a million battles and always win as I'm the idealistic hero, successful and all I want to be, I often wonder if dreams do come true, I hope they do.

Enough about myself, seeing the new way I express myself why don't you have a go too? Just sit down and think about yourself; who are you in different circumstances? Which part of you do you like best?

I found this a very emotional time for me, so don't give in and please do share your end result with me.

I look forward to hearing from you,

P.S. Please reply soon.

Denise Pounds

My Life

My-Anh Tran-Dang

My picture portrays my past, present and future; I have concentrated specifically on events which happened in my past because it changed my life completely. The cruel Vietnam War had divided my family and I have expressed that in a powerful image.

The first time I saw my father was when I was five years old, the snowflakes in the picture are significant to my imagery; it was Christmas when my mother, brother and I arrived in England to be with my father, and it was the very first time I have seen snow. Each and every snowflake is beautiful and precious; I have put a picture of my family, reunited at last, in the centre of a snowflake, so it is symbolic. From then on, we started a whole new life together.

At present I am working hard for my career and future prospects. I have included my interests and hobbies too (astrology, palm-reading, Tae-kwon-do).

I believe that we should make the most of our lives; to take every opportunity that comes our way. I think that the events in my life have made me somewhat stronger and determined; I hope to fulfill my dreams and aspirations.

After all, life is too short and precious to waste.

Achievements

Practical skills. Pupils acquired a range of new skills, in particular those concerned with composition and use of materials.

> Everything different can join together and work out alright.
> (I learnt that) ... you can blend colours and shapes together

> You don't need to use conventional materials you can use anything.

Critical skills. The fact that Allan showed, did and talked about his own work enabled pupils to develop a greater understanding of what he was trying to say and of how he was trying to say it.

> His work is political – it affects his life.

> He is trying to present that there is hope.

> He tries to show family bonds and troubles in his paintings.

Taking risks. Visual artists and writers rarely have an image or a text in their heads waiting to pour out onto canvas or paper. More often than not, they begin with a draft or sketch, then they rework, making additions and deletions. Their ideas develop in the process so that pupils seeing artists working in this way can gain confidence and begin to work like this themselves. It is not always easy for pupils to take risks and make mistakes. An artist working in the classroom can provide an excellent role model and source of inspiration.

> I learnt not to be afraid to experiment and not to worry about messing my work up.

> I learnt not to worry about mistakes .... and to keep trying to create a better and realistic setting without trying again on a different paper.

Cross-curricular work. Not all of the pupils worked with both the writer and the artist, but it is quite clear from their work that those who did have this opportunity were able to benefit from taking ideas from one subject to the other.

> At first I found it quite difficult (in art) and I didn't have any ideas about what I could do, but after a while I found it easier - having a writer in my English lesson helped.

Talking about racism. The arts (visual, written and performance) can be a very effective source and vehicle for enabling pupils to explore political and personal issues in the classroom. The arts can help pupils to empathise, and to identify with new experiences and to make sense of difficult ones.

> It is important to talk about issues like stereotyping and about the dangers (of this).

> I am non–European and I share Allan's feelings that some people in this country are racist towards us.

> Allan's work made me think differently about (people from) different countries and how their life is. I didn't realise that they are under so much pressure and under attack as constantly as they are.

Presenting ourselves. This can sometimes be painful. It is important therefore for an atmosphere to be created whereby pupils can say that they find the activity difficult or intrusive and alternatives to be provided.

> I don't really want to carry on with the work I'm doing because I don't want everyone knowing about me and my past life.

> I don't like talking about my private life.

Others felt that they hadn't lived long enough or just didn't have enough to say:

> I liked the idea. My only problem is that nothing special has happened in my life.

> I find it difficult expressing myself....I can't think of new and interesting ways of doing it.

Some pupils, on the other hand, found the exercise stimulating and thought-provoking and were very honest and self critical in their work:

> After working with (the artists) I think more deeply about my past and present and more about what I would like to do in the future.

> I find it more difficult talking about myself and putting it into a picture as a story of my life. I have never done anything like this before so it was a bit harder than normal art lessons.

> I have learnt a lot about myself, feeling new emotions and finding out that I'm not really the person I thought I was.

Planning your own Residency

Working with an artist can be a valuable and rewarding experience for pupils and for the teacher, but unless it is carefully planned it can be a wasted opportunity. It may be helpful to bear in mind the following points in your planning:

Pre-planning

- why do you want to work with an artist?
- what are your aims and objectives?
- find out about possible artists from Regional Arts Association (RAA), AEMS Project, Arts and Crafts Council, local arts centres, Minority Arts Advisory Service (MAAS), Commonwealth Institute. There are a number of registers of artists available (see resources section at the end of this chapter) and it is worth consulting them
- match your own needs with the artists available.
- avoid stereotyping the artist, allow them to describe their work and ideas to you
- draw up a short-list of artists – consider art form, content, approach, style, experience of working in schools
- identify sources of funding (approximately £80.00 a day plus travel). You can contact your LEA, RAA, AEMS

- contact/meet with the artist.
- agree on the artist for the residency
- make a formal application for funding

Planning

- meet with the artist at the school to plan the residency
- exchange address/telephone numbers
- agree on the respective roles of the teacher and the artist
- confirm the dates and times of the residency
- identify the area where the artist will be working
- what materials are required? Order materials
- are there any special requirements, e.g. access to a dark room?
- which pupils will the artist work with? (Don't try to spread the artist too thinly across too many pupils)
- insurance – if the artist is leaving his/her work at the school make sure that it is covered by insurance
- make a timetable for the artist
- make sure that the artist has some time during the day to get on with his/her own work where appropriate
- build in time for the artist to talk to the pupils and staff about his/her own work
- allow time each day to talk with the artist and review the residency
- make sure that the rest of the school know as much about the residency as possible, for example introducing the artist to the school in an assembly, ensuring all staff know the artist, disseminating information about the artist and his/her work
- make links with other teachers and departments in the school. It may be that the English teacher could work with the visual artist or at least make links through the pupils' work.
- agree outcomes, for example performance, exhibitions, publications etc
- confirm all planning with the artist in writing
- plan your method of evaluation

The residency

- continually review the residency. Be honest with the artist. It is far better if you have concerns about the work to discuss them openly
- evaluate the impact of the residency in as many ways as possible. Interview pupils about their work, ask pupils to keep diaries, discuss the residency with the artist and with colleagues, look at pupil's work etc
- document the residency, keep pupils' work, take photographs, videos etc This can assist the evaluation process; it can also help in further applications for funding

Follow up

- evaluation is essential, not just for those directly involved, i.e. the artist and

the teacher, but also for the school as a whole, school governors, parents etc. It is worth spending time on a written report
- it is important to let the rest of the school know about the residency, through a newsletter, exhibition, presentation, etc
- let the artist know of any feedback from pupils or any publications, exhibitions or documentation. Artists are keen to know about the longer term impact of their work
- follow up the work of the artist through reviews, visits to exhibitions, performances etc
- check the artist has been paid

Outside the European tradition

Artists working alongside teachers in the classroom offer a range of new skills and learning experiences to both pupils and teachers. A particular feature of the AEMS residencies, of course, is that they give children the opportunity of working alongside artists working from outside the European tradition. There are many additional benefits which derive from the new skills and varied approaches which such artists bring with them. The following list has been adapted from a diagram devised by Maggie Semple, Director of the AEMS Project:

- *Catalysts of change.* New ideas and approaches can create a climate of change in which pupils and teachers may feel more able to develop and experiment in their work.
- *Role models.* Black artists drawing on contemporary and traditional art forms from a range of cultural backgrounds provide positive role models for all pupils.
- *Different approaches.* The role of the artist in society is culturally determined, thus artists from different cultural backgrounds offer new ways of working.
- *Arts within a cultural context.* Artists are able to present ideas and information about themselves and their artform which provides a cultural context in which their work is placed.
- *New skills.* Artists are able to introduce skills which are not usually a part of the curriculum.
- *Challenging assumptions and stereotypes.* Artists challenge assumptions and stereotypes through their work in schools and through the content of their work.
- *Cross-curricular work.* Artforms are not in themselves 'discrete' and the divisions between the arts are culturally determined. For example, in some non-European cultures dance and music are not seen as distinct arts activities. Thus, non-European artists can provide natural opportunities for cross-curricular work.
- *Legacy.* The impact of the residency can be long-lasting, in terms of memories, skills and artefacts.

References

Dhingra, L. (1987) *Watchers and Seekers*. London: Women's Press.
Dhingra, L. (1988) *Amritvela*. London: Women's Press

Resources

Organizations

African and Asian Visual Artists Archive. Comprehensive archive of African and Asian artists working in Britain, containing a collection of slides, posters, catalogues, press cuttings and biographical material. Contact: AAVAA, The Coach House, Small Business Centre, 2 Upper York Street, Bristol, BS2 8QN. Tel: 0272 244492

Art and Development Education Project. A London-based curriculum development project. Contact: Top Floor, Effra School, Barnwell Road, Brixton, London SW2 1PL. Tel: 071 737 7967 or 071 326 1883

Arts Education for a Multicultural Society Project. AEMS is a national curriculum development project. The project has developed a number of excellent resources. Contact: Maggie Semple, Project Director, AEMS, The Commonwealth Institute, Kensington High Street, London W8 6NQ. Tel: 071 603 4535, ext 242.

Commonwealth Institute, Kensington High Street, London W8 6NQ. Tel: 071 603 4535. In addition to a permanent exhibition, the Commonwealth Institute operates a library loan service of books and artefacts. They can also provide advice and information about the work of Commonwealth artists.

Minority Arts Advisory Service. Offers advice and information on the work of artists from a variety of cultural backgrounds. Contact: 28 Shackwell Lane, 4th Floor, London E8 2EZ. Tel: 071 254 7295

Museum of Mankind. Museum exhibition and resource centre with education programme. Contact: Ben Burt, Education Department, Museum of Mankind, Burlington Gardens, London W1X 2EX. Tel: 071 437 2224

Regional Arts Associations. Your local Regional Arts Association can offer advice, resources and financial assistance to schools interested in working with artists.

Publications

Arts Education for a Multicultural Society (AEMS)(1990) *Resources for Arts Education in a Multicultural Society.* London: AEMS.

Arts Education for a Multicultural Society (AEMS) (1990) *The AEMS Directory of Artists for Education.* London: AEMS.

Afro-Caribbean Education Resource Centre (1989) *Resource and Information Guide.* 3rd edition. Afro-Caribbean Education Resource Centre, Wyvil

School, Wyvil Road, London SW8 2TJ

Dust, K. and Sharp, C. (1990) *Artists in School: A Handbook*. London: Bedford Square Press.

The National Curriculum Council Arts in Schools Project (1990) *The Arts 5–16 Project Pack*. Edinburgh: Oliver and Boyd

INDEX